THE ENGLISH BOOK TRADE

SKETCHES OF SOME

BOOKSELLERS

OF THE TIME OF

DR. SAMUEL JOHNSON

.

SKETCHES OF SOME

BOOKSELLERS

OF THE TIME OF

DR. SAMUEL JOHNSON

BY

E. MARSTON

[1902]

AUGUSTUS M. KELLEY • PUBLISHERS
CLIFTON 1972

First Edition 1902

(London: Sampson Low, Marston & Company Ltd., *St. Dunstan's House,* 1902)

920.4
A57s

Reprinted 1972 by

Augustus M. Kelley Publishers

REPRINTS OF ECONOMIC CLASSICS

Clifton New Jersey 07012

I S B N 0 678 00727 6

L C N 79 107923

74 3803

PRINTED IN THE UNITED STATES OF AMERICA

by SENTRY PRESS, NEW YORK, N. Y. 10013

SKETCHES OF SOME
BOOKSELLERS
OF THE TIME OF
DR. SAMUEL JOHNSON

Samuel Johnson, LL.D.
After an Engraving by E. Finden.

SKETCHES OF SOME
BOOKSELLERS

OF THE TIME OF

DR. SAMUEL JOHNSON

BY

E. MARSTON

AUTHOR OF "SKETCHES OF BOOKSELLERS
OF OTHER DAYS," ETC. ETC.

" Sir, I always said the Booksellers were a generous
set of men. . . . The fact is, not that they have paid me
too little, but that I have written too much."
DR. JOHNSON.

LONDON

SAMPSON LOW, MARSTON & COMPANY, LTD.

ST. DUNSTAN'S HOUSE

1902

I dedicate this book to my dear Granddaughter

DOROTHIE DANIELS,

because she says I must do so, and her must *is equal to a Queen's command. She tells me frankly that she does not care a bit for musty old booksellers of centuries ago; but then, she is very good to one old bookseller of to-day, and so it comes to pass that I send her this book, on my seventy-eighth birthday, with my love.*

E. M.

St. Valentine's Day, 1902.

CONTENTS

LIST OF PORTRAITS, ETC.

NOTE.

T has been a source of pleasure to me to look up scraps of information here and there about the old Booksellers. My first volume of "Sketches," published last year, was so indulgently received that I have been tempted once again to bring together into this volume a further series which appeared from time to time in "The Publishers' Circular." I have added much matter to each sketch, whilst the last four chapters appear here for the first time. All the Booksellers herein mentioned were more or less known to Dr. Johnson, or had important business transactions with him. It is for this reason that I have associated Dr. Johnson's name on the title-page with those who were from circumstances brought into personal contact with him. "If," says Charles

Knight, "Samuel Johnson was the Jupiter of
Literature during fifty years of the eighteenth
century, the Booksellers of that period, with
whom he had familiar intercourse, literary and
social, were his satellites." I have endeavoured
in every case to give the salient points in the
story of each man's life, and in pursuit of the
needful material I am greatly indebted to that
learned and genial old literary gossip Mr. John
Nichols, as well as to Mr. James Boswell, and
to Dr. Johnson himself. But for these authorities very little indeed would now be known of
the Booksellers of the Eighteenth Century:
"Some of the most eminent of whom," says
Mr. Knight, "from the days of Pope to those
of Cowper belong to a period which may justly
be called the *Johnsonian Era.*" I hope I have
not wholly failed in presenting in a readable
form these old Booksellers of a century and a
half ago to the Booksellers and other readers
of the Twentieth Century.

E. M.

London,
February 14, 1902.

SKETCHES OF SOME BOOK-SELLERS OF THE TIME OF DR. JOHNSON

I. MICHAEL JOHNSON OF LICH-FIELD, 1656-1731

THE house in which Michael John-son carried on his business as a bookseller, and in which Samuel Johnson, his son, was born in 1709, has become the property of the City of Lichfield, through the generosity of Lieut.-Colonel John Gilbert, who some time ago bought and presented it to his native place. On Satur-day, July 6th, 1901, it was opened by Dr. Birk-beck Hill as a Museum and Library. Members

of the London Johnson Club attended the cere-
mony, and were received by the Mayor and
Corporation, and an oration was delivered in
the large hall of the Bishop's Palace by Mr.
Augustine Birrell, K.C., and a Johnson sermon
was preached in the cathedral by the Rev.
Canon Lonsdale.   The house was built by
Michael Johnson on land belonging to the
Corporation, in whose records there appears
this entry, under date July 13th, 1708 :

"Agreed that Mr. Michael Johnson, bookseller, have a lease of his encroachment of his
house in Sadler Street, and Women's Cheaping,
for forty years, at 2s. 6d. per annum."

Boswell has preserved the particulars of a proceeding in which the bailiffs and citizens, to their
great honour, on the expiration of a second
lease in 1767, resolved that it should be renewed to Samuel Johnson for a further term of
ninety years at the old rent, and without pay-
ment of any fine.

Michael Johnson was born at Cubley, in
Derbyshire, in 1656.   But little or nothing is
known of his ancestors.   Dr. Johnson once said
to Boswell, " I have great merit in being zealous
for the honours of birth, for I can hardly tell

MICHAEL JOHNSON.

Born in 1656; died in 1731.

*From an engraving by E. Finden after the original drawing
in the possession of Mr. John Murray.*

[To face page 2.

who was my grandfather." He settled in Lichfield as a bookseller and stationer. He married
Sarah Ford, who was born at King's Norton,
Worcestershire, in 1669, and who was descended
from an ancient race of substantial yeomanry in
Warwickshire. They were well advanced in
years, he being over fifty and she over forty [1]
when they married ; they had two children, both
sons, Samuel, their first-born, who lived to be
the world-renowned Doctor Samuel Johnson,
and Nathaniel, who died in his twenty-fifth [2]
year.

In the register of St. Mary's Parish Church,
Lichfield, is recorded the baptism of Samuel on
September 18th, N.S., 1709. Michael, the
father, is there styled "Gentleman." Croker
says :

" The title Gentleman had still in 1709 some
degree of its original meaning, and as Mr.

[1] So says Mrs. Piozzi ; but as Michael was born in
1656, and Samuel, his son, in 1709, he would have been
fifty-two, and as his wife was born in 1669 she could
not have been more than thirty-nine when they were
married.

[2] Mrs. Piozzi says that Nathaniel died at the age of
twenty-seven or twenty-eight. Malone in a footnote
says he was born in 1712 and died in 1737—he was
therefore not more than twenty-five when he died.

Johnson served the office of Sheriff of Lichfield in that year, he seems to have been fully entitled to it.   The Doctor, at his entry on the books of Pembroke College, and at his matriculation, designated himself as *filius generosi.*"

One of his godfathers was Dr. Swinfen, a physician of the city.   Three years after the baptism of his brother is thus entered in the same Register :

"Oct. 14, 1712.   Nathaniel, son of Mr. Michael Johnson, baptized."

Mrs. Piozzi says of Michael Johnson, doubtless from information gathered from his son, that he was a very pious and worthy man, but wrong-headed, positive, and afflicted with melancholy : his business, however, leading him to be much on horseback, contributed to the preservation of his bodily health and mental sanity, which, when he stayed long at home, would sometimes be about to give way; when his workshop, a de-tached building, had fallen down for want of money to repair it, his father was not less dili-gent to lock the door every night, though he saw anybody might walk in at the back part and knew that there was no security obtained by barring the front door.

Michael was a man of still larger size and greater strength than his son, who was reckoned very like him.

On July 19th, 1712, he was elected a magistrate and brother of the Incorporation of Lichfield, and on the 25th he took the oath of allegiance, and that he believed there was no transubstantiation in the Sacrament of the Lord's Supper.

Mr. Croker says:

"There seems some difficulty in arriving at a satisfactory opinion as to Michael Johnson's real condition and circumstances. That in the latter years of his life he was poor is certain; and Dr. Johnson not only admits the fact of *poverty*, but gives several instances of what may be called *indigence*. Yet, on the other hand, there is evidence for nearly fifty years he occupied a respectable rank amongst his fellow-citizens, and appears in the annals of Lichfield on occasions not bespeaking poverty. . . . In 1709 (the year of Samuel's birth) Michael Johnson served the office of Sheriff of the County of the City of Lichfield. In 1718 he was elected junior bailiff, and in 1725 senior bailiff or chief magistrate. Thus respected and apparently thriving in Lichfield, the following extract of a letter written by the Rev. George Paxton, Chaplain to Lord Gower, will show the high estimation in which the father

of our great moralist was held in the neighbouring county :

"'Trentham, St. Peter's Day, 1716.—Johnson,
the Lichfield Librarian, is now here; he propa-
gates learning all over this Diocese, and ad-
vanceth knowledge to its just height; all the
clergy here are his pupils, and suck all they have
from him; Allen cannot make a warrant without
his precedent, nor our quondam John Evans
draw a recognisance *sine directione Michaelis.*'"

During the two years which Samuel Johnson
passed at home before proceeding to Oxford,
he was engaged in learning his father's business,
and it is said that books of his binding are still
extant in Lichfield—but he did not take kindly
to that business. "Once," said he, "I was dis-
obedient. I refused to attend my father to
Uttoxeter market. Pride was the source of that
refusal, and the remembrance of it was painful.
A few years ago I desired to atone for this fault.
I went to Uttoxeter in very bad weather, and
stood for a considerable time bare-headed in the
rain on the spot where my father's stall used to
stand. In contrition I stood, and I hope the
penance was expiatory."

In Dr. Johnson's account of his early life I
find a scrap about his father which does not in-
dicate poverty :

"My father being that year Sheriff of Lichfield, had to ride the circuit of the county next day, which was a ceremony then performed with great pomp; he was asked by my mother, 'Whom he would invite to the Riding?' and answered 'All the town now.' He feasted the citizens with uncommon magnificence, and was the last but one that maintained the splendour of the Riding."

At that time he must have been in affluent circumstances, but these declined as he grew older. Boswell says:

"He was forced by the narrowness of his circumstances to be very diligent in business, not only in his shop, but by occasionally resorting to several towns in the neighbourhood, some of which were at a considerable distance from Lichfield. At that time, booksellers' shops in the provincial towns of England were very rare, so that there was not even one in Birmingham, in which town old Mr. Johnson used to open a shop every market day. He was a pretty good Latin scholar, and a citizen so creditable as to be made one of the magistrates of Lichfield; and being a man of good sense, and skill in his trade, he acquired a reasonable share of wealth, of which, however, he afterwards lost the greatest part, by engaging, unsuccessfully, in a manufacture of parchment."

In the year 1705 there was published a little volume, now very scarce, entitled "An Account of the Life of Dr. Samuel Johnson, from his birth to his eleventh year, written by himself." (Boswell's "Life of Johnson," vol. i.)

From this Account I am induced to give the following interesting particulars, having reference both to his father and his mother:

"Sept. 7, 1709, I was born at Lichfield. I was born almost dead, and could not cry for some time. In a few weeks an inflammation was discerned on my buttock, which was at first, I think, taken for a burn ; but soon appeared to be a natural disorder. It swelled, broke, and healed. . . . I was by my father's persuasion put to one Marelew, to be nursed. Here it was discovered that my eyes were bad, and an issue was cut in my left arm. . . . My mother visited me every day, and used to go different ways that her assiduity might not expose her to ridicule. . . .

"In ten weeks I was taken home, a poor diseased infant, almost blind. I remember my Aunt Nath. Ford told me when I was about . . . years old, that she would not have picked such a poor creature up in the street. . . . My father and mother had not much happiness from each other. They seldom conversed ; for my father could not bear to talk of his affairs ; and my mother, being unacquainted with books, cared not to talk of anything else. Had my mother been more literate, they had been better company. In Lent, 1712, I was taken to London, to be treated for the evil of Queen Anne. My

mother was at Nicholson's, the famous bookseller in Little Britain. . . . We went in the
stage coach, and returned in the wagon, as my
mother said, because my cough was violent.
The hope of saving a few shillings was no
slight motive; for she not having been accustomed to money, was afraid of such expenses
as now seem very small. She sewed two guineas
in her petticoat lest she should be robbed. We
were troublesome to the passengers."

Michael Johnson does not seem to have published much. I have only heard of two books
bearing his imprint, viz. :

" An Exposition of the Revelations by shew-
ing the agreement of the prophetick symbols
with the History of the Roman, Saracen and
Ottoman Empires, and of the Popedom. To
this are added Remarks on this prophecy. The
work is dedicated to the Rt. Rev. Father in
God, Edward Lord Bishop of Litchfield and
Coventry. By John Floyer. London : *Printed
for M. Johnson, Bookseller, Lichfield, in* 1719."

This pamphlet is very scarce. The one from
which I copied this title was lent to me by
Mr. Rupert Simms of Newcastle-under-Lyme.

And in the catalogue of William Salt, Esq.
(for the sight of which I am also indebted to
Mr. Rupert Simms), I find the following :

"Bradley (J.).   Impartial View of the Truth of Christianity, with Life and Miracles of Apollonius Tyanæus (very scarce).   *Printed by W. Downing for M. Johnson.*   Lichfield, 1699."

Of course there may be many other books bearing Mr. Michael Johnson's imprint during his long career as a bookseller, but the above are the only titles I have met with.   His business was chiefly that of a bookseller and stationer.   He travelled about from town to town with a stock of books, which he sold by auction.

The following is the title-page and address to his customers of one of Michael Johnson's sale catalogues.   I quote it in full, as it illustrates the way in which books were disposed of in country places nearly 200 years ago, and I think it will be read with interest by those booksellers and others of to-day who are not already acquainted with it.

"A catalogue of choice books, in all faculties, divinity, history, travels, law, physic, mathematics, philosophy, poetry, etc., together with bibles, common-prayer books, shop-books, pocketbooks, etc.   Also fine French prints, for staircases, and large chimney-pieces ; maps large and small.   To be sold by auction, or he who bids most, at the Talbot, in Sidbury, Worcester. The sale to begin on Friday the 21st of this instant March, 1717-18, at six o'clock in the afternoon, and to continue till all be sold. Catalogues are given out at the place of sale, or by Michael Johnson of Lichfield.

" To all Gentlemen, Ladies, and others in and near Worcester :—I have had several auctions in your neighbourhood, as Gloucester, Tewkesbury, Evesham, etc., with success, and am now to address myself and try my fortune with you.

" You must not wonder that I begin every day's sale with small and common books ; the reason is, a room is some time a filling ; and persons of address and business seldom coming first, they are entertainment till we are full ; they are never the last books of the best kind of that sort, for ordinary families and young persons, etc. But in the body of the catalogue you will find law, mathematics, history ; and for the learned in divinity : there are Drs. South, Taylor, Tillotson, Beveridge, Flavel, etc., the best of that kind ; and to please the ladies, I have added store of fine pictures and paperhangings ; and, by the way, I would desire them to take notice, that the pictures shall always be exhibited by the noon of that day they are to be sold, that they may be viewed by daylight.

" I have no more, but to wish you pleased, and myself a good sale, who am your humble servant,
" M. JOHNSON."

Michael Johnson died at the age of seventy-six of an inflammatory fever, and his wife of gradual decay at the age of eighty-nine.

"The Gentleman's Magazine," October, 1829, has the following account of the business after Michael's death :

"After her husband's decease, Johnson's mother continued the business, though of course on a more contracted scale. Among the names of subscribers to the 'Harleian Miscellany' there occurs that of 'Sarah Johnson, Bookseller, in Lichfield.' The humble nature of her establishment may be gathered from a passage in Miss Seward's Correspondence, where she says of Lucy Porter : 'From the age of twenty she boarded in Lichfield with Dr. Johnson's mother, who still kept that bookseller's shop by which her husband supplied the scanty means of existence. Meantime, Lucy kept the best company of our little city, but would make no engagement on market days, lest Granny, as she called Mrs. Johnson, should catch cold by serving in the shop. There Lucy took her place, standing behind the counter, nor thought it a disgrace to thank a poor person who purchased from her a penny battledore.' "

I have been favoured by Mr. J. T. Raby, of "The Staffordshire Advertiser," with the sight of a work entitled "Graphic Illustrations of the Life and Times of Samuel Johnson, LL.D." (John Murray, 1837). In this volume is a fine engraving by E. Finden of Michael Johnson

THE HOUSE IN WHICH SAMUEL JOHNSON WAS BORN.

From an engraving by E. Finden after a drawing in the possession of Mr. John Murray.

[To face page 12.

from a drawing in the possession of Mr. John
Murray. I have now the pleasure of giving a
reproduction of this portrait. There is not
much in the text which accompanies the portrait
beyond what I have already supplied from other
sources. I may add that the volume which
Mr. Raby has lent me is somewhat scarce; the
many engravings in it are very fine. It is
destined for the library of " The Johnson House,"
now the property of the City of Lichfield.

Saturday, July 6th, 1901, was a memorable
day at Lichfield; for it was on that day that the
Johnson Museum and Library were dedicated
to the public by that enthusiastic Johnsonian,
Dr. Birkbeck Hill. The London members of
the Johnson Club visited the city on the occasion, and were received with all enthusiam by
the city authorities. Dr. Birkbeck Hill in his
speech dedicated the house as " a shrine to all
Johnsonians," and there seems to be a probability that Lichfield may become such a shrine
more increasingly in the future than it has been
in the past.

It may be interesting to our friends in " the
Row " and elsewhere to be reminded that the
Johnson Club was founded by our *confrère*, Mr.

Fisher Unwin, in December, 1884, on the centenary of Dr. Johnson's death.

Among the members of the Johnson Club was Mr. Augustine Birrell, K.C., who delivered an interesting lecture at the Palace, in which he told a story about Johnson which does not appear to have got into print before. " Mrs. Sherwood's mother while on a visit to Lichfield met Johnson under the trees in the Close. The poor young lady congratulated herself, for she held in her hand a volume of 'The Rambler.' He took the book from her hand to remark what she was studying. So soon as he discovered what it was he threw it among the graves and stalked away ! " It seems to have been a bearish action on the part of the Doctor —which is as much as can be said for it.

Mr. Birrell concluded his lecture by saying that they were there " to commemorate a great man, a great character, whose works, character, and genius would be as well known 117 years hence as they were then."

This reminds me of a similar remark quoted, I think, by Croker, in 1831 : " Johnson will have more readers and admirers in 1901 than he has now."

II. ANDREW MILLAR, 1707-1768

NDREW MILLAR," says Nichols, "was literally the artificer of his own fortune. By consummate industry and a train of successive patronage and connection he became one of the most eminent booksellers of the eighteenth century." He was as popular as he was prosperous. He had little pretension to learning, but he had a thorough knowledge of mankind and a nice discrimination in selecting his literary counsellors, among whom it may be sufficient to mention the late eminent schoolmaster and critic, Dr. William Rose of Chiswick, and the late William Strahan, Esq., his early friend and associate in private life, and his partner in many capital adventures in business.

" Mr. Boswell in his ' Life of Johnson ' says of Millar that, ' though himself no great judge of literature, he had good sense enough to have for his friends very able men to give him their opinion and advice in the purchase of copyrights; the consequence of which was his acquiring a very large fortune, with great liberality.' "

Johnson said of him, " I respect Millar, Sir, he has raised the price of literature."

Andrew Millar was born in Scotland in 1707. I have been unable to trace his early career, but I find that he established himself in business in 1729 near St. Clement's Church, at No. 141 in the Strand.   He afterwards removed to Tonson's old shop, " The Shakespeare's Head," which he rechristened " The Buchanan's Head," opposite to Catherine Street.

" Here," says Knight, " Andrew Millar concluded, over many a hospitable entertainment in his upper rooms, his treaties with Fielding and Thomson, with Hume and Robertson.   Here Thos. Cadell wrote to Gibbon to tell him how wonderful was the success of ' The Decline and Fall of the Roman Empire.' "

In 1729 he paid Thomson £137 10s. for " Sophonisba " and " Spring," and in 1738 £105 for sole right for " The Seasons."   He paid Fielding £183 10s. for " Joseph Andrews," and for "Tom Jones" £600, and an additional £100, and in 1751 £1,000 for "Amelia." Mallet is said to have refused his offer of £3,000 for the copyright of Bolingbroke's Works—and a fortunate refusal it was for Millar. The editor had afterwards to borrow money of Millar to get the book printed. Mr. Knight says that Mallet published, at his own risk, Bolingbroke's Works in five volumes quarto, and Davies says that the edition was not sold off in twenty years.

When Lord Bolingbroke died in 1751, he left all his writings, published and unpublished, to Mallet. The fact has been preserved from oblivion by Johnson's invective that one scoundrel loaded a blunderbuss and left another half-a-crown to fire it off.

Among Millar's many great literary undertakings not the least was that of the publication of Dr. Johnson's "Dictionary of the English Language," in which he held a large share. The prospectus of this great work was announced to the world in the year 1747. The booksellers who contracted with Johnson, single and unaided, for the execution of the work, were Mr. Robert Dodsley, Mr. Charles Hitch, Mr. Andrew Millar, the two Messrs. Longman, and the two Messrs.

Knapton. The price agreed was *fifteen hundred and seventy-five pounds*. The work was to have been completed in three years, but it does not appear to have been completed till the year 1755. Mr. Millar took the principal charge of conducting the publication of the Dictionary, "and as," says Boswell, "the patience of the proprietors was repeatedly tried and almost exhausted by their expecting that the work would be completed within the time which Johnson had sanguinely supposed, the learned author was often goaded to dispatch, more especially as he had received all the copy money, by different drafts, a considerable time before he had finished his task.

"When the messenger who carried the last sheet to Millar returned, Johnson asked him, 'Well, what did he say?'

"'Sir,' answered the messenger, 'he said, Thank God I have done with him.'

"'I'm glad,' replied Johnson, 'that he thanks God for anything.'"

In a footnote referring to the above Boswell says that "Sir John Hawkins in *his* life of Johnson mentions two notes as having passed formally between Millar and Johnson to the above effect; but he had been assured that this was not the case—two notes would have been *morose*, whereas in the way of incidental remark it was a pleasant play of raillery."

It was in the year 1736 that a society was established under the title of "The Society for the Encouragement of Learning." It came out under sufficiently exalted auspices, the Duke of Richmond being its first president, and Brian Fairfax, Esq., vice-president, Sir Hugh Smithson, afterwards Duke of Northumberland, and Sir Thomas Robinson, Bart., trustees. The committee of management numbered twenty-four, and embraced the names of many noblemen and gentlemen of the first rank in literature, among whom were the Earl of Hertford, Earl of Aberdeen, Earl of Oxford, Earl Stanhope, etc., and as secretary Mr. Alex. Gordon, at a salary of £50 a year, and they started with 102 members.

With such an array of talent, great things in the way of literary productions may well have been looked for, and the Society started full of ambition and hope.

It was at the time regarded as a direct attack on the booksellers; but it was soon found that their aid could not be dispensed with, and a contract for three years was entered into with Andrew Millar, J. Gray, and J. Nourse to act as their distributors.

Looking back on the Society now, after an interval of a century and a half, one cannot help feeling that it was not altogether fortunate in its first secretary, if one may be allowed to judge him by the spirit and tone of his letter addressed to the Rev. Dr. Richardson, Master of Emmanuel College, Cambridge, which letter was written in his zeal to forward the interests of his Society. The letter is given in full in Nichols's "Literary Anecdotes." I will only quote a few passages which will sufficiently show the pomposity, the assumption of dignity, and the haughty scorn of this terrible secretary. The letter is dated London, December 8th, 1736, and from it one can gather the nature of the institution and the motives which suggested it.

"We are every day increasing both in numbers and in members either conspicuous for their quality and station, or learning and ingenuity ; next, as I have the honour of serving them in the quality of their Secretary I own I never saw any committee better attended, nor more unanimity among any set of men. They had already entirely paved the way for the reception of authors; appointed booksellers for their service; settled the regulations concerning printers and the printing part, being determined to spare neither pains nor charges in what they shall publish, so that it may be done in the most elegant and beautiful manner. In fine, nothing is wanting but to set out with some author of genius and note, in order to give the publick a specimen of their desire to serve them as well as the author. Several authors have already applied, but the Committee have laid it down as a rule not to set out but with the work of some man of genius and merit in English: wherefore as the ingenious Dr. Middleton of Cambridge is about 'The Life of Cicero' I should be obliged if you would take an opportunity to acquaint him that if he does our Society the favour to let them publish it, I dare venture to assure him that it will be received with honour. I shall add that in point of interest it will be a little estate to the author whose works they begin with, for every mortal will buy it. . . . You have no doubt heard in what a discouraging way Dr. Bentley has used our Society; for though his work of 'Manilius' was ready to be printed, and he desired by several people to have it published by the Society, he not only raised such illgrounded objections against the institution itself, but chose to throw it into the hands of a common bookseller, rather than those of the Society, which has not only made several gentlemen of letters and high life exclaim against the discouraging and ungenerous act, but will be recorded to the learned world, perhaps, when he is dead and rotten. Such men deserve fleecing from booksellers; and I am mistaken if he or his editors will not meet with it; I am sure none will regret them. But it is hoped, nay expected, from the excellent character Dr. Middleton bears in the world, that our Society will meet with other treatment from him, for it is as much the duty of a great Author to lend a helping hand to encourage and countenance so laudable an Institution as is that of this Society, as it is for the Society to encourage the Author."

Dr. Middleton does not seem to have listened to the voice of this charmer. Nor would James Thomson desert his old friend Andrew Millar, who had published "The Seasons" in 1730 and continued to be his publisher till the issue of his last poem, "The Castle of Indolence," in 1748.

Nichols says: "However liberal the idea of such an institution might have been, the execution of it counteracted the intention of the founders. It was (as has already been said) a direct attack on the booksellers, who, after all, are certainly no bad rewarders of literary merit."

"This Mr. Gordon," says Nichols, "made trial of all the ways by which a man could get an honest livelihood." He was the author of

several works of travel and antiquarian interest,
the chief of which was " Itinerarium Septentrionale, or a Journey through most of the Counties
of Scotland." He resigned his position as
secretary of the Society for the Encouragement
of Learning in 1739. In 1741 he went to
Carolina, where he purchased the office of
Registrar of the Province, and died a Justice of
the Peace, leaving a handsome estate to his
family. It was "Sandy" Gordon's " Itinerarium
Septentrionale " that the " Antiquary " had just
purchased and was examining with so much
pride " from title-page to colophon " when he
was riding in Mrs. Machleuchar's coach from
Edinburgh to Queensferry, which was timed to
start at twelve o'clock. Monkbarns did not
arrive till ten minutes late, exclaiming, " Deil's
in it, I am too late after all ! " But the coach
had not arrived; then followed the wrathful
call of the " Antiquary," which brought Mrs.
Machleuchar up the stairs exclaiming, " The
coach ! gude guide us, gentlemen, is it no on
the stand yet ? Is it the coach ye hae been
waiting for ? "

In 1742 a third method was adopted, and
the Society chose to become their own pub-

lishers.   The experiment was tried with Ælian,
" De Animalibus," 4to, in 1743.   A few months
were sufficient to demonstrate the impractic-
ability of the attempt, and before the year was
at an end they again had recourse to the booksellers.   By 1745 their finances had become
almost exhausted, and by 1748 they had in-
curred so considerable a debt as to be deterred
at that time from proceeding further in their
project of printing.

Mr. Millar seems to have had a good deal of
practical experience in the matter of *copyright*.
It had been assumed that, notwithstanding the
Statute of Queen Anne, 1709 (8, c. 19), which
secured the author for fourteen years, and
another term of fourteen years if the author
were living, making twenty-eight years in all,
that copyright once obtained was held in perpetuity.   Andrew Millar held the copyright of
Thomson's " Seasons," but according to the
statute it had expired.   The work was issued by
Taylor, against whom Millar brought an action
in 1766, which was decided by the Court of
King's Bench in 1769 in Millar's favour, on the
ground that the Common Law Copyright was
unaffected by the Statute of Queen Anne.

This decision was subsequently reversed in the case of Donaldson *v.* Beckett, and it was affirmed that perpetual copyright was taken away by the Statute of Queen Anne.

Andrew Millar had three children, but they all died in their infancy. "He was not extravagant," says Nichols, "but contented himself with an occasional *regale* of humble port at an opposite tavern, so that his wealth accumulated rapidly."

As a curious comment on this remark of Nichols I find the following in Boswell's "Life of Johnson":

"Dr. Johnson, talking of the effects of drinking, remarked: 'A bookseller who got a large fortune by trade was so habitually and equably drunk, that his most intimate friends never perceived that he was more sober at one time than another.'"

A footnote by Croker says: "This was Andrew Millar, of whom, when talking one day of the patronage the great sometimes affect to give to literature and literary men, Johnson said, 'Andrew Millar is the Mæcenas of the age.'"

He was very fortunate in his trade assistants. One of them was Robert Lawless, a name familiar to every bibliomaniac and to every book-

seller of the time.   He was for more than half a
century well known to and much distinguished
by the notice of many of the most eminent
literary characters of his time, as one of the
principal assistants, first to Mr. Millar, then to
Mr. Cadell, and finally to Cadell and Davies.
He died in 1806 at the age of eighty-two.

" A purer spirit," says Nichols, " never in-
habited the human bosom.   One instance of his
singleness of heart may be given.   Not very
long before Mr. Cadell obtained the scarlet
gown, on taking stock at the end of the year
honest Robin very seriously applied to his
master, to ask a favour of him.   Mr. Cadell, of
course, thought it might be something beneficial
to the applicant, but great was his surprise to
find that the purport of his request was *that his
annual salary may be lowered, as the year's
account was not so good as the preceding one.*"

It was in 1758 that Millar met with an apprentice, Mr. Cadell, congenial to his most
ardent wishes, who became his partner seven
years afterwards in 1765, and in 1767 he relinquished the whole business to him.

Andrew Millar now retired to a villa at Kew
Green, and died the following year, and was
buried in the cemetery at Chelsea, where in
1751 he had erected an obelisk over a vault

appropriated to his family, where three infant children were deposited, and where afterwards his own remains and those of his widow, who had been re-married to Sir Archibald Grant, Bart., were also deposited. She left many charitable benefactions : among others the whole residue of her estate (at least £15,000) to be disposed of at the discretion of her three executors—the Rev. Dr. Trotter, Mr. Grant, and Mr. Cadell.

III. THOMAS DAVIES, 1712-1785

T was said of Davies that he was "not a bookseller, but a gentleman who dealt in books." He was also a gentleman who played many parts in the drama of life, first as an actor, then as a bookseller, author, and dramatist. Mr. Nichols gives a long account of his career, and it is largely from this source and from the immortal Boswell that I have gathered what follows.

He was born in the year 1712, in Edinburgh. He completed his education at the University of Edinburgh, and became, as Dr. Johnson used to say of him, "learned enough for a clergyman."

"He was," says Nichols, who knew him intimately, "a man of uncommon strength of mind, who prided himself on being through life a companion of his superiors."

He seems to have manifested an early taste for the stage, and his name appears in 1736 among the *dramatis personæ* of Lillo's celebrated tragedy "Fatal Curiosity," at the theatre in the Haymarket, where he was the original performer of young Wilmot, under the management of Henry Fielding. He also performed at Edinburgh, where he was manager of the theatre. Through his superior acting, he appears while there to have given umbrage to, and aroused the jealousy of, his brethren, which led to much acrimonious correspondence in the Scotch newspapers.

Not succeeding to his hopes on a London stage, he became an itinerant, and performed at York, where he married Miss Yarrow, daughter of an actor there, whose beauty was not more remarkable than her private character was ever unsullied and irreproachable.

In none of these callings was he particularly successful in a commercial sense, whether as actor, bookseller, or author; but he always retained the esteem and affection of many friends;

he was truly indebted to his good friend Dr. Samuel Johnson for many acts of generous kindness, and many alleviations when he was in sore distress.   He left the stage, when he and his wife were making five hundred a year, from a very thin-skinned sensitiveness.   It was owing to a critical poem by Churchill, referring to his acting :

" He mouths a sentence, as curs mouth a bone."

" But," says Johnson, " what a man is he who is to be driven from the stage by a line ! Another line would have driven him from his shop."

In a short time he commenced business as a bookseller, in Duke's Court, opposite the church of St. Martin-in-the-Fields, and afterwards in Round Court, near the Strand ; but he met with misfortunes in trade, and again returned to the stage, and on January 24th, 1746, " Venice Preserved " was acted for his benefit at Covent Garden Theatre.

Thomas Davies told Boswell that Johnson was very much his friend, and came frequently to his house.   " He was," says Boswell, " a man of good understanding and talents, with the ad-

vantage of a good education ; and his literary
performances have no inconsiderable share of
merit.   He was a friendly and very hospitable
man.   Both he and his wife, who was celebrated for her beauty, and who, though upon
the stage for many years, maintained an uni-
form decency of character." Churchill, in "The
Rosciad," says of her :

"... on my life,
That Davies has a very pretty wife."

It was in Davies's back parlour, where Boswell was taking tea with him and Mrs. Davies,
that Boswell first became acquainted with Dr.
Johnson.   Boswell was but twenty-two at the
time (1763), and he regarded it as a memorable
year, for then it was that he first knew that
extraordinary man whose memoirs he wrote—
"An acquaintance," says he, "which I shall
ever esteem as one of the most fortunate circumstances of my life."

Davies, perceiving the great Doctor in his
shop through the glass door in the room in
which they were sitting, announced his awful
approach somewhat in the manner of an actor
in the part of Horatio, when he addresses

Hamlet on the appearance of his father's ghost :

"Look, my lord, it comes."

Mr. Davies respectfully introduced Mr. Boswell, who was greatly agitated, to the formidable Doctor.

He whispered to Davies, "Don't tell where I come from." "From Scotland," cried Davies, roguishly. "Mr. Johnson," said Boswell "I do indeed come from Scotland, but I cannot help it."

This, of course, was said not as a humiliating abasement at the expense of his country, but as a light pleasantry, which he thought would soothe and conciliate the Doctor. The speech, however, was somewhat unlucky. He seized the expression, "Come from Scotland," and retorted, "That, sir, I find is what a very great many of your countrymen cannot help." This was a stunning stroke for Boswell, and he sat down not a little embarrassed, and apprehensive of what might come next.

Johnson, turning to Davies, remarked: "What do you think of Garrick? He has refused me an order for the play for Miss Williams because he knows the house will be full and that an order would be worth three shillings."

Mr. Boswell, eager to seize any opening to get into conversation with him, ventured to say :

"O, sir, I cannot think Mr. Garrick would grudge such a trifle to you."

"Sir," said he with a stern look, "I have known David Garrick longer than you have done, and I know no right you have to talk to me on the subject."

This was certainly a rough extinguisher for young Boswell, who began to think that the hope which he had long indulged of obtaining his acquaintance was blasted. "And in truth," said he, " had not my ardour been uncommonly strong, and my resolution uncommonly per-severing, so rough a reception might have deterred me for ever from making any further attempts." Boswell remained upon the field and listened for some time to the wisdom which fell from the Doctor's lips, and was enabled now and then to make an observation, which he received very civilly. On leaving, Davies followed him to the door, and comforted him for the hard blows which the great man had given him by saying, "Don't be uneasy; I can see he likes you very well."

A few days afterwards Boswell called on Davies and asked him if he thought he might take the liberty of waiting on Mr. Johnson at his chambers in the Temple. He said he certainly might, and that Mr. Johnson would take it as a compliment. He called accordingly, and was received very courteously.

Thus it was that Tom Davies, the bookseller, was the means of bringing together these two men, of whom it may be said that if they had never met, the world would have been deprived of the most charming and most unique record of a great man's life that has ever been produced. Without Boswell, Johnson's great name would have been hidden and overshadowed long ago except to the learned few. Without Johnson, Boswell's name would never have been heard of. The result of the combination of their names has been the production of a work which the world will not easily let die.

Davies recollected several of Johnson's remarkable sayings, and was one of the best imitators of his voice and manner.

Boswell says: "Johnson's laugh was as re-

markable as any circumstance in his manner.
It was a kind of good-humoured growl." Tom
Davies described it drolly enough, " He laughs
like a rhinoceros."

On one occasion, however, he presumed too
much on his intimacy with the great man.
During Johnson's absence on his celebrated
" Tour to the Hebrides," Davies, in his capacity
as a publisher, took the unpardonable liberty
of publishing two volumes, entitled " Miscellaneous and Fugitive Pieces," which he adver-
tised in the newspapers as being " By the
Author of ' The Rambler.' " [1] In this collection several of Dr. Johnson's writings, several
of his anonymous performances, and some
which he had written for others were inserted,
and also some with which the Doctor had
no concern whatever. He was at first very
angry, as he had good reason to be. But
upon consideration of his poor friend's narrow
circumstances, and that he had only a little
profit in view, and meant no harm, he soon
relented, and continued his kindness to him
as usual. Mrs. Piozzi gives an amusing ac-

[1] A third volume was subsequently added, presumably
with the Doctor's sanction.

count of this little episode, which I am tempted
to quote :

"'How,' said I, 'would Pope have raved
had he been served so!' 'We should never,'
replied Johnson, 'have heard the last on't, to
be sure ; but then Pope was a narrow man.   I
will, however,' added he, 'storm and bluster
myself a little this time ;' so went to London,
in all the wrath he could muster up.   At his
return I asked how the affair ended.   'Why,'
said he, 'I was a fierce fellow, and pretended
to be very angry, and Thomas was a good-
natured fellow, and pretended to be very sorry;
so *there* the matter ended.   I believe the dog
loves me dearly.   Mr. Thrale (turning round to
my husband), what shall you and I do that is
good for Tom Davies?   We will do something
for him, sure. '"

Of course this was an impudent invasion of
Dr. Johnson's copyright, and in the hands of a
less kindly disposed person than Dr. Johnson
would have proved extremely awkward for Tom
Davies.   Curiously enough, Boswell subsequently quotes the case of the Rev. Mr.
Mason's prosecution of Mr. Murray (for there
was a John Murray in those days, the great-
grandfather of the present John).   Mr. Murray
had inserted in a collection of " Gray's Poems "
only fifty lines, of which Mr. Mason had still

the exclusive property, under the Statute of Queen Anne. Mr. Mason persevered, notwithstanding his being requested to name his own terms of compensation. (It was fortunate for Davies that he had Johnson and not Mason for his antagonist.)

Dr. Johnson expressed his dipleasure at Mason's conduct very strongly; but added, by way of showing that he was not surprised at it, ' Mason 's a Whig." Mrs. Knowles (not hearing distinctly): "What, a prig, sir?" Johnson: "Worse, madam, a Whig! But he is both!"

This question of *literary copyright* was at this time in a doubtful position as to whether the common law did not give copyright in perpetuity, notwithstanding the statute of Queen Anne. Johnson, writing to Boswell, February 7th, 1774, says:

"The question of *literary property* is this day before the Lords. Murphy drew up the appellant's case—that is, the plea against the perpetual right. I have not seen it, nor heard the decision. *I would not have the right perpetual.*"

Croker, in a footnote, says:

"The question was not decided till February

22.   In consequence of this decision the English
booksellers have now no other security for any
literary purchase they may make but the statute
of the 8th of Queen Anne, which secures to the
author's assigns an exclusive property for fourteen years, to revert again to the author, and
vest in him for fourteen years more."

"Not meeting with that success," says Nichols,
"which his attention and abilities merited, Mr.
Davies, in 1778, was under the disagreeable
necessity of submitting to become a bankrupt,
when such was the regard entertained for him
by his friends that they readily consented to his
re-establishment . . . but all their efforts might
have been fruitless if his great and good friend
Dr. Johnson had not exerted all his interest in
his behalf."

Johnson did all he could to befriend him.
He called upon all who had any influence to
assist Tom Davies, and prevailed on Mr. Sheridan, patentee of Drury Lane Theatre, to let
him have a benefit, which he granted on the
most reasonable terms.   In a letter to Mrs.
Montagu he writes :

"Now, dear Madam, we must talk of business.   Poor Davies, the bankrupt bookseller, is
soliciting his friends to collect a small sum for
the repurchase of some of his household stuff.
Some of them gave him five guineas.   It would
be an honour to him to owe part of his relief to
Mrs. Montagu."

In another letter he writes to the same lady :

" Madam,—I hope Davies, who does not want wit, does not want gratitude, and that he will be almost as thankful for the bill, as I am for the letter that enclosed it."

At a much earlier date, 1765, Boswell found the following entry in Johnson's Diary, which shows him in a very amiable light :

" July 16.—I received seventy-five pounds, lent Mr. Davies twenty-five."

In 1780, by a well-timed publication, " The Life of Mr. Garrick," in two volumes, which passed through four editions, Davies not only acquired fame but realized money.

In a critique on this work in " The Gentleman's Magazine " the reviewer concludes :

" We shall now take our leave of Messrs. Garrick and Davies's performance with a distich analogous to what has been said of Richardson the printer :

' If Booksellers thus cleverly can write,
Let writers deal in books and booksellers indite.' "
NICHOLS, *Lit. Anec.*, vol. vi.

In 1780 Johnson, writing to Dr. Beattie, says : " Mr. Davies has got great success as an author, generated by the corruption of a bookseller." This has reference to "Memoirs of David Garrick," by Thomas Davies.

On this Croker remarks:

"What the expression 'generated by the corruption of a bookseller' means seems not quite clear; perhaps it is an allusion to the generation of a certain class of insects, as if Davies, from his adversity as a bookseller, had burst into new and gaudier life as an author."

It is an expression that wanted elucidation, and this is, perhaps, as good as any other.

In the year 1783 I find the following letter written by Dr. Johnson to Mr. Davies:

"June 18, 1783.

"Dear Sir,—I have had, indeed, a very heavy blow; but God, who spares my life, I humbly hope will spare my understanding and restore my speech. As I am not at all helpless, I want no particular assistance, but am strongly affected by Mrs. Davies's tenderness; and when I think she can do me good, shall be very glad to call upon her. I had ordered friends to be shut out, but one or two have found their way in; and if you come you shall be admitted; for I know not whom I can see that will bring more amusement on his tongue, or more kindness in his heart.

"I am, etc.,
"SAM. JOHNSON."

Boswell adds to this :

" It gives me great pleasure to preserve such a memorial of Johnson's regard for Mr. Davies, to whom I was indebted for my introduction to him. He, indeed, loved Davies cordially, of which I shall give the following little evidence :—One day, when he had treated him with too much asperity, Tom, who was not without pride and spirit, went off in a passion ; but he had hardly reached home when Franks, who had been sent after him, delivered this note :

" ' Come, come, dear Davies, I am always sorry when we quarrel ; send me word that we are friends.' "

In 1784 Johnson wrote the following letter to him :

" August 14.

" To Mr. Thomas Davies,

" The tenderness with which you always treat me makes me culpable in my own eyes for having omitted to write in so long a separation. I had, indeed, nothing to say that you could wish to hear. All has been hitherto misery accumulated upon misery, disease corroborating disease, till yesterday my asthma was perceptibly and unexpectedly mitigated. I am much comforted with this short relief, and am willing to flatter myself that it may continue and improve. I have at present such a degree of ease as not only may admit the comforts but the duties of life. Make my compliments to Mrs. Davies. Poor dear Allan![1] He was a good man."

It was in 1762, a few years before he finally quitted the stage, that he resumed his former occupation of a bookseller in Russell Street, Covent Garden.

In 1772 he collected and republished the pastoral poems of William Browne and the poems of Sir John Davies, and in 1773 he brought out the volume of " Miscellaneous and Fugitive Pieces, by the Author of 'The Rambler,'" which brought down upon him the wrath of Dr. Johnson. In 1774 he published the works of Dr. John Eachard, late Master of Catharine Hall, Cambridge. In 1777 he was the author of " The Characters of George the First, Queen Caroline, etc., with Royal and Noble Anecdotes," 12mo.

In 1779 he published, and apparently wrote, " Some Account of the Life and Writings of Massinger," prefixed to a new edition of his works in four volumes. It was inscribed to Dr. Samuel Johnson "as a small but sincere tribute to his liberal and extensive learning, his great

---

[1] Allan Ramsay, painter to his Majesty.

and uncommon genius, and his universal and active benevolence."

In 1780 he wrote and published the "Life of David Garrick," already referred to.

Mr. Davies was the writer of numberless essays in prose and verse in the "St. James's Chronicle" and other public newspapers. Nichols says that he knew Davies well, and "for several years passed many convivial hours in his company at a social meeting,[1] where his lively sallies of pleasantry were certain to entertain his friends by harmless merriment. The last time, however, that he visited them he wore the appearance of a spectre ; and, sensible of his approaching end, took a solemn valediction. Poor ghost ! how it would comfort thee to know that, at a subsequent meeting of thy sincere friends, the impression of thy last appearance was not eradicated; and that every breast heaved a sympathetic sigh, lamenting the loss of so excellent an associate."

He died May 5th, 1785, aged about seventy-three. He was buried by his own desire in the

---

[1] This was at "The Booksellers' Literary Club," held at "The Devil Tavern" and subsequently at "The Shakespeare." See Sketch No. VII.

vault of St. Paul's, Covent Garden, and the following lines were written on the occasion :

> "Here lies the author, actor, Thomas Davies,
> Living, he shone a very *rara avis*.
> The scenes he play'd life's audience must commend,
> He honoured Garrick, Johnson was his friend."

Mrs. Davies, his widow, died February 9th 1801.

IV. THOMAS OSBORNE, DIED 1767

HOMAS OSBORNE, although he was, as Dibdin says, "the most celebrated bookseller of his day," seems to have had little claim from any personal merit to the esteem of his contemporaries ; and if he had any desire that his name should be carried down and be remembered by future generations, it would hardly have been that he should be specially distinguished as the man whom Dr. Johnson knocked down with a folio volume, placed his foot on his breast, and exclaimed " Lie there, thou son of dulness, ignorance, and obscurity."

I have been unable to gather any information as to Osborne's birth or early career, except

that he was the son of Thomas Osborne, who
carried on business as a stationer in Gray's Inn,
and died in 1743. He left his stock, copyrights,
etc., to his son Thomas. When he first came
into notice he was carrying on a very large and
prosperous bookselling and publishing business
in Gray's Inn. The first mention of him by
Boswell is that he " supposed Johnson to be
the author of an advertisement for Osborne,
concerning the great Harleian Catalogue."

Dibdin, in his " Bibliomania," says :

" Of Tom Osborne I have in vain endeavoured
to collect some interesting bibliographical de-
tails. What I know of him shall be briefly
stated. He was the most celebrated bookseller
of his day ; and appears from a series of his
catalogues in my possession to have carried on
a successful trade from the year 1738 to 1768
[1767 ?]. He was for many years one of the
Court of Assistants of the Stationers' Company,
and died August 21st, 1767. His collections
were truly valuable, for they consisted of the
purchased libraries of the most eminent men
of those times. In his stature he was short and
thick, and to his inferiors generally spoke in an
authoritative and insolent manner. In the latter
part of his life his manners were considerably
softened, particularly to young booksellers who
had occasion to frequent his shop in pursuit of
their orders. If they were so fortunate as to

call whilst he was taking wine after his dinner
they were regularly called into the little parlour
in Gray's Inn to take a glass with him. 'Young
man,' he would say, 'I have been in business
more than forty years, and am now worth
more than forty thousand pounds. Attend
to your business, and you will be as rich as
I am.' "

Dibdin lamented that Osborne acquired the
library of the Earl of Oxford "to the irreparable
loss, and I had almost said the indelible dis
grace of the country." It was, however, no
disgrace to Osborne that he should have had
the pluck, the good judgment, and above all
the ready money to put down such a large sum
as £13,000 for this great collection, and Dibdin
seems to have begrudged Osborne what seemed
on the face of it to be the very great bargain he
had made; but it should be remembered that
Osborne had to realize his money by selling
out in small driblets during probably a period
of years what he had bought and paid for in a
lump. It was said that the *binding* alone of
only a portion of the stock acquired by Osborne
had cost Lord Oxford £18,000.

In the year 1743-4 there was issued an
account of this celebrated collection under the

title " Catalogus Bibliothecæ Harleianæ," in
four volumes, and we learn from Boswell that
Dr. Johnson was employed " by Osborne to
write the preface," "which," says Boswell, " he
has done with an ability that cannot fail to im-
press all his readers with admiration of his
philological attainments."   Dibdin, however,
not being under the spell of the great doctor,
as Boswell always was, differed from him ; he
says, " in my humble apprehension the preface
is unworthy of the doctor ; it contains a few
general philological reflections, expressed in a
style sufficiently stately, but is divested of bibliographical anecdote and interesting intelligence."

For the first two volumes of the catalogue
Osborne had charged 5s. each, which was resented by the booksellers as an avaricious in-
novation.   He was also accused of rating his
books at too high a price ; to which he replied :

" If I have set a high value upon books, if I
have vainly imagined literature to be more
fashionable than it really is, or idly hoped to
revive a taste well-nigh extinguished, I know
not why I should be persecuted with clamour
and invective, since I shall only suffer by my
mistake, and be obliged to keep the books I
was in hopes of selling."

The foregoing paragraph does not read like the composition of an ignoramus such as Dibdin and Johnson have represented him to have been; but as a matter of fact it is said to have been written by Johnson himself; it is also a proof that they were at that time—which seems to have been subsequent to the knock-down blow—on a friendly footing.

The booksellers were unreasonable in their complaint of high prices, and, indeed, it appears that Osborne's prices were extremely moderate, and the sale of the books so very slow that Johnson assured Boswell "there was not much gained by the bargain."

In an article on "The Progress of Sale Catalogues" by Richard Gough, 1788, Nichols's "Lit. Anec.," vol. iii., p. 65, he writes:

"Among these Catalogists stands foremost Tom Osborne, who filled one side of Gray's Inn with his lumber, and without knowing the intrinsic value of a single book, contrived such arbitrary prices as raised him to his country-house and dog-and-duck huntings."

Osborne's advertisements, which were sometimes inserted in the "London Gazette," were drawn up in the most ridiculously vain and

ostentatious style; in them he was to tell the
"publick" that he possessed "all the pompous
editions of Classicks and Lexicons."

Sir John Hawkins tells the story at large of
Johnson's knocking Osborne down with a folio
volume, and prefaces it by the following severe
delineation of his character.

"Osborne was an opulent tradesman, as may
be judged from his ability to make so large a
purchase as the Earl of Oxford's Library.   He
was used to boast that he was worth £40,000;
but of Booksellers he was one of the most ig-
norant; of title-pages and editions he had no
knowledge or remembrance, but in all the
tricks of the trade he was most expert.   Johnson in his 'Life of Pope' says that he was entirely destitute of shame, without sense of any
disgrace but that of poverty.   His insolence to
customers was sometimes past bearing."

Osborne appears in "The Dunciad" contend-
ing for the prize among booksellers, and carries
it off:

"Osborne, through perfect modesty o'ercome,
Crown'd with the jordan, walks contented home."

OSBORNE KNOCKED DOWN WITH A FOLIO.

Here is the whole story as given in the
"Life of Samuel Johnson, LL.D.," published by

G. Kearsley, 1785, and quoted in "John-soniana":

"Tom Osborne, the bookseller, was one of 'that mercantile rugged race to which the delicacy of the poet is sometimes exposed,'[1] as the following anecdote will more fully evince. Mr. Johnson being engaged by him to translate a work of some consequence, he thought it a respect which he owed to his own talents, as well as the credit of his employer, to be as circumspect in the performance of it as possible. In consequence of which, the work went on, according to Osborne's ideas, rather slowly; he frequently spoke to Johnson of this circumstance; and, being a man of a coarse mind, sometimes by his expressions made him feel the situation of dependence. Johnson, however, seemed to take no notice of him, but went on according to the plan which he had prescribed to himself. Osborne, irritated by what he thought an unnecessary delay, went one day into the room where Johnson was sitting, and abused him in the most illiberal manner; amongst other things, he told Johnson 'he had been much mistaken in his man; that he was recommended to him as a good scholar, and a ready hand, but he doubted both; for that Tom such-a-one would have turned out the work much sooner, and that being the case, the probability was that by this *here* time the first edition would

---

[1] Johnson's "Life of Dryden."

have moved off.' Johnson heard him for some time unmoved; but, at last losing all patience, he seized a huge folio which he was at that time consulting, and, aiming a blow at the bookseller's head, succeeded so forcibly as to send him sprawling on the floor. Osborne alarmed the family with his cries; but Johnson, clapping his foot on his breast, would not let him stir till he had exposed him in that situation; and then left him with this triumphant expression: ' Lie there, thou son of dulness, ignorance, and obscurity.' "

In volume viii. of Nichols's " Literary Anecdotes," p. 446, it is confidently stated that the identical book with which Johnson felled Osborne was " Biblia Græca Septuaginta," folio, 1594, Frankfort. A note written by the Rev. — Mills states that he saw this work at Cambridge in February, 1812, in the possession of J. Thorpe, bookseller, whose catalogue, since published, contains particulars authenticating the assertion.

It was this Thomas Osborne in conjunction with Charles Rivington who proposed to Richardson to write the volume of " Familiar Letters " from which sprang " Pamela." Osborne was rather a bookseller than a publisher; he appears to have been very successful in the purchase of private libraries and in issuing elaborate catalogues of the same.

At one time he had a partner, for I find the following in Richard Gough's " Progress of Sale Catalogues " : "Sale by Shropshire, at Exeter-'change, on announcing dissolution of partnership between T. Osborne and J. Shipton, three parts and pamphlets." In Nichols's "Anecdotes," vol. viii., p. 463, there is also mention of Osborne and Shipton's "Catalogue of the Libraries of the Right Honourable Henry Lord Viscount Coleraine, the Honourable Mr. Baron Clarke, and many others, containing 200,000 volumes of the most scarce and valuable Books in all Languages, Arts and Sciences, viz., the pompous editions of the Greek and Roman Classicks, etc., etc." The sale was to be continued daily for two years, from November, 1754, to November, 1756. The catalogue was in two large volumes. The D. N. B. says that in 1754 he was in partnership with J. Shipton, and had taken a house at Hampstead. His name appears on the title-page as a shareholder of many works of the period in connection with several other publishers, as was the custom in those days, and which indeed was continued down to the middle of the last century, when it gradually died out. It seems to have been a good and wise custom, inasmuch as it was calculated to promote friendly and sociable relations between publishers, discouraged ruinous rivalry, and reduced individual risk to a minimum. On the other hand, even when the profits of a work were large, when divided among a large number of shareholders each individual's share did not amount to much. So it gradually came about that each publisher, making haste to be rich, began to think it more to his own interests to " paddle along in his own canoe," and to take upon himself the burden of all losses and the solace of all profits ; and thus it has happened that in the course of time there has been a great increase in the number of publishers, each one bent on the keenest rivalry with his neighbours, and with doubtful benefit to any one. This rivalry was destructive of the old sociability, every man's hand being against his brother. It brought about a kind of anarchy which flourished during the greater part of the nineteenth century. The end of that century has seen the establishment of an Authors' Association, a Publishers' Association, and a

Booksellers' Association, and these together, it is reasonable to hope, will lead to the advancement of literature and the prosperity of all interested in its production.

Osborne died August 21st, 1767, and was buried on the 27th at St. Mary's, Islington.

V. BERNARD LINTOT, 1674-1735
AND
HENRY LINTOT, 1709-1758
(FATHER AND SON)

ERNARD was the son of John Lintot, of Horsham in Sussex, yeoman. The date of his birth is not given, but as he died at the age of sixty-one, in the year 1735, he must have been born about 1674. Nor have I found any account of his boyhood or his early education. He was about sixteen when he was bound apprentice at Stationers' Hall to Thomas Lingard, December 4th, 1690—turned over to John Harding 169-, and made free March 18th, 1699.

Dunton says of this Mr. Harding: "Without flattery, he deserves to be called a very courteous man, of a lovely proportion, extremely well made, as handsome a man, and as good an air, as perhaps few of his neighbours exceed him."

Bernard Lintot, soon after his freedom, commenced business as a bookseller, October 13th, 1700, at the sign of "The Cross Keys and Crown," next Nando's Coffee House, the first house east of Temple Lane, where he was patronized by many of the most eminent writers of a period which has been styled the Augustan Age of English Literature.

He was married at St. Bartholomew's, Smithfield, to one Catherine, who was born in 1664; a son Henry was born in 1709.

Among his earliest publications was a work by Thomas D'Urfey, gentleman, in 1704, entitled "Tales, Tragical and Comical." Judged by their titles, these tales were of a licentious or scandalous character. Dunton says of them and of the publisher: "Lintot lately published a collection of tragic tales, by which I perceive he is angry with the world, and scorns it into the bargain; and I cannot blame him, for

D'Urfey both treats it and esteems it as it deserves; too hard a task for those whom it flatters, or perhaps for Bernard himself, should the world ever change its humour, and *grin* upon him. However, to do Mr. Lintot justice, he is a man of very good principles, and I dare engage will never want an author of *Sol-fa*, as long as the playhouse will encourage his comedies."

In 1709 he published "Oxford and Cambridge Miscellany Poems," and in 1714 he reprinted the Miscellanies, with several poems by Mr. Pope, also by Dryden, Swift, Gay, etc. The same year he entered into a very liberal agreement with Mr. Pope for his translation of Homer's "Iliad," the printing of which was undertaken by Mr. William Bowyer the elder.

It was about this time, when evidently the author and publisher were on very good terms —that is, between the months of September, 1715, and February, 1716—that Mr. Pope wrote a most amusing though rather sarcastic letter (evidently not intended for publication) to the Earl of Burlington, in which he describes his old friend Bernard Lintot, and, although the letter is well known and has been frequently quoted, I make no apology for quoting it again nearly at its full length. "I know nothing in our language," says Dr. Warton, "that equals it":

"My Lord; if your mare could speak, she would give you an account of what extraordinary company she had on the road; which since she cannot do, I will. It was the enterprising Mr. Lintot, the redoubtable rival of Mr. Tonson, who, mounted on a stone-horse (no disagreeable companion to your Lordship's mare), overtook me in Windsor Forest. He said he heard I designed for Oxford, the seat of the Muses, and would, as my bookseller, by all means, accompany me thither.

"I asked him where he got his horse? He answered he got it of his Publisher;[1] for that rogue, my printer (said he), disappointed me; I hoped to put him in good humour by a treat at the tavern, of a brown fricassee of rabbits, which cost two shillings, with two quarts of wine, besides my conversation. I thought myself cocksure of his horse, which he readily promised me, but said that Mr. Tonson had just such another design of going to Cambridge, expecting there the copy of a new kind of Horace from Dr. ——, and if Mr. Tonson went he was pre-engaged to attend, being to have the printing of the said copy. 'So in

---

[1] Lintot being himself a *publisher*, this probably means some one in his employ.

short, I borrowed this stone-horse of my Publisher, which he had of Mr. Oldmixon for a debt; he lent me, too, the pretty boy you see after me; he was a smutty dog yesterday, and cost me near two hours to wash the ink off his face; but the Devil is a fair-conditioned Devil, and very forward in his catechise; if you have any more bags he shall carry them.' I gave the boy a small bag, containing three shirts and an Elzevir Virgil; and mounting in an instant proceeded on the road, with my man before, my courteous stationer beside, and the aforesaid Devil behind.

"Mr. Lintot began in this manner: 'Now, d—— them! what if they should put it into the newspapers, how you and I went together to Oxford? what would I care? If I should go down into Sussex, they would say I was gone to the Speaker. But what of that? If my son were but big enough to go on with the business, by ——— I would keep as good company as old Jacob.'[1]

"Hereupon I inquired of his son. 'The lad,' says he, 'has fine parts, but is somewhat sickly, much as you are. I spare for nothing in his Education at Westminster. Pray, don't you think Westminster to be the best school in England? Most of the late Ministry came out of it, and so did many of this Ministry. I hope the boy will make his fortune.'

"'Don't you design to let him pass a year at Oxford?' 'To what purpose?' (said he). 'The

[1] Jacob Tonson.

Universities do but make Pedants, and I intend
to breed him a man of business.'

"As Mr. Lintot was talking, I observed he
sat uneasy on his saddle, for which I expressed
some solicitude. 'Nothing,' says he, 'I can
bear it well enough : but since we have the day
before us, methinks, it would be very pleasant
for you to rest awhile under the woods.' When
we were alighted, 'See here what a mighty
pretty Horace I have in my pocket! what if
you amused yourself by turning an Ode, till we
mount again? Lord! if you pleased, what a
clever Miscellany might you make at leisure
hours?' 'Perhaps I may,' said I, 'if we ride
on, the motion is an aid to my fancy, a round
trot very much awakens my spirits ; then jog on
apace, and I'll think as hard as I can—'

"Silence ensued for a full hour, after which
Mr. Lintot hugged the reins, stopped short, and
broke out : "Well, sir, how far have you gone?'
I answered seven miles. 'Zounds, sir,' said
Lintot, 'I thought you had done seven stanzas.
Oldisworth, in a ramble round Wimbleton-Hill,
would translate a whole Ode in half this time.
I'll say that for Oldisworth (though I lost by
his Timothy's), he translates an ode of Horace
the quickest of any man in England. I remember Dr. King would write verses in a
tavern three hours after he could not speak ;
and there's Sir Richard, in that rumbling old
chariot of his, between Fleet Ditch and St.
Giles' Pond, shall make you half a *Job*.'

"'Pray, Mr. Lintot' (said I), 'now you talk
of translators, what is your method of managing

them?' 'Sir' (replied he), 'those are the sad-
dest pack of rogues in the world; in a hungry
fit, they'll swear they understand all the languages in the universe; I have known one of
them take down a Greek book upon my counter,
and cry, "Ah! this is Hebrew, I must read it
from the latter end." By —————— I can never
be sure in these fellows, for I neither understand Greek, Latin, French, nor Italian myself.
But this is my way.   I agree with them for 10s.
per sheet, with a proviso that I will have their
doings corrected by whom I please; so by one
or other they are led at last to the true sense of
an author; my judgment giving the negative to
all my translators. . . . I'll tell you what happened to me last month; I bargained with
S—— for a new version of Lucretius, to publish
against Tonson's; agreeing to pay the author
so many shillings at his producing so many
lines.   He made great progress in very short
time, and I gave it to the corrector to compare with the Latin; but he went directly
to Creech's translation, and found it the same
word for word, all but the first page.   Now
what d'ye think I did? I arrested the translator
for a cheat; nay, and I stopped the corrector's
pay too, upon the proof that he had made use
of Creech instead of the original.'
    " 'Pray tell me next how you deal with the
Critics?'   'Sir,' said he, 'nothing more easy.
I can silence the most formidable of them; the
rich ones for a sheet apiece of the blotted
manuscript, which cost me nothing; they'll go
about with it to their acquaintance, and pre-

tend they had it from the author, who submitted it to their correction; this has given some of them such an air, that in time they come to be consulted with, and dedicated to as the top Critics of the Town. As for the poor Critics,' says he, ' I'll give you one instance of my management by which you may guess at the rest.

" ' A lean man, that looked like a very good scholar, came to me t'other day ; he turned over your Homer, shook his head, shrugged his shoulders, and pish'd at every line of it ; "One would wonder," says he, "at the strange presumption of some men : Homer is no such easy task, that every stripling, every versifier"—he was going on, when my wife called to dinner; "Sir," said I, "will you please eat a piece of beef with me?" " Mr. Lintot," said he, " I am sorry you should be at the expense of this great book ; I am really concerned on your account." " Sir, I am obliged to you ; if you can dine upon a piece of beef, together with a slice of pudding—" " Mr. Lintot, I do not say but Mr. Pope, if he would condescend to advise with men of learning—" " Sir, the pudding is upon the Table, if you please to go in." My critic complies, he comes to a taste of your poetry, and tells me in the same breath, that the book is commendable, and the pudding excellent.' . . .

" A. POPE."

Nichols quotes from a small memorandum book entitled " Copies when purchased," which had been kept between the years 1701 and 1724 by the Lintots. This memorandum book was discovered by D'Israeli. A few extracts from it, with reference to Pope's " Homer," may be of interest to publishers of to-day.

MR. POPE.

	£	s.	d.
1714, Mar. 23. HOMER, Vol. I. .	215	0	0
650 books on royal paper	176	0	0
1716, Feb. 9. HOMER, Vol. II. .	215	0	0
650 copies on royal paper	150	0	0
1717, Aug. 9. HOMER, Vol. III.	215	0	0
650 copies on royal paper	150	0	0
1718, Mar. 3. HOMER, Vol. IV.	210	0	0
650 copies on royal paper	150	0	0
1718, Oct. 7. HOMER, Vol. V. .	210	0	0
1719, April 6.			
650 copies on royal paper	150	0	0
1720, Feb. 26. HOMER, Vol. VI.	210	0	0
May 7.			
650 copies on royal paper	150	0	0
Paid Mr. Pope for the subscription money due on the second volume of Homer, and on his fifth volume, at the agreement for the said fifth volume . .	840	0	0

£ s. d.

(I had Mr. Pope's assignment for
the royal paper copies that were
then left of his Homer.)

Copy money for the "Odyssey,"
Vols. I., II., III., and 750 of
each volume printed on royal
paper 4to 615 0 0

Copy money for "Odyssey," Vols.
IV. and V., and 750 of each vol.
roy. 4to 425 18 7½

Sundry other works . . . 162 10 0
_____
4,244 8 7½

Another curious entry in the "Mcmorandum
Book" is as follows :

"'1722, Oct. 24. A copy of an agreement
for purchasing 250 of the Duke of Bucking-
ham's works—*afterwards Jockeyed by Alderman
Barker and Tonson together.*' A footnote says,
'Who can insure Literary Celebrity? No
Bookseller would *now* regret being *Jockeyed* out
of his Grace's works.'"—D'ISRAELI.

Dr. Johnson, in his "Life of Pope," says :

"The highest bidder (for Pope's 'Homer')
was Bernard Lintot, who became proprietor, on
condition of supplying, at his own expense, all

the copies which were to be delivered to subscribers, or presented to friends, and paying £200 for every volume. . . . The subscribers were 575. The copies for which subscriptions were given were 654. For these copies Pope had nothing to pay; he therefore received, including the £200 a volume, £5,320 without deduction, as the books were supplied by Lintot."

The above entries in the "Memorandum Book" do not complete the payments if, as Johnson says, Pope received £5,320.

The work proved an immediate success as to numbers of copies sold, but it appears not to have been altogether profitable to Lintot. Nichols says:

"It is unpleasant to relate that the bookseller, after all his hopes and all his liberality, was, by a very unjust and illegal action, defrauded of his profit.[1] An edition of the 'Iliad' was printed in Holland in duodecimo, and imported clandestinely for the gratification of those who were impatient to read what they could not yet afford to buy. This action compelled Lintot to bring out a still cheaper edition, which seems to have had a very large

[1] This could hardly have been, for the publication is said to have laid the foundation of Lintot's fortune.— Ed.

sale, but at a price so low as not to be profitable."

Charles Knight says:

" Pope gained nearly £3,000 by the 'Odyssey,' but Lintot was disappointed, and pretended that there was something fraudulent in the agreement, and threatened a suit in Chancery. Pope quarrelled of course with him."

Presumably this sum of £3,000 means the profits made by Pope on his subscriptions as well as what Lintot paid him.

In the severe frost of January and February, 1715-16, the River Thames was one solid block of ice, and shops of every description were erected on its surface. Amongst these, printers and booksellers were also found pursuing their professions. Lintot seems to have been there.

" In this place Bowyer plies, that's Lintot's stand."
DAWKS's *News Letter.*

Mr. Nichols in a short notice of Mr. John Bagford, who was a great authority on the history and art of printing, says that he also practised the art, which is shown by two cards printed on the frozen River Thames. In the area of one of these cards, in capital letters, are

"Mr. John Bagford" and the four following lines :

> "All you who walk upon the Thames,
> Step in this booth, and print your names,
> And lay it by, that ages yet to come
> May see what things upon the Thames were done."

"Printed upon the frozen River Thames Jan. 18, 1715-16."

Bernard Lintot, as may be gathered from Pope's description of him, must have been of a jovial, sociable nature, not particularly thin-skinned, and mighty shrewd in all the concerns of his business. He soon acquired a competency, and added to his paternal inheritance in Sussex. He seems to have been desirous of tracing the origin of his family, and consulted the custodian of the Earl of Oxford's Heraldic MSS., Mr. Humphrey Wanley, in whose diary was found the following memorandum :

"Young Mr. Lintot, the Bookseller, came inquiring after *arms* as belonging to his father, mother, and other relations, who, now it seems want to turn *Gentlefolks*. I could find none of their names." [1]

---

[1] Arms were granted, 1723, to *Thos.* Lintot of Wadhurst. It does not appear whether he was of the same family as the bookseller.

Up to this point, the completion of the publication of Pope's Homer, that is until about
1725, there seems to have been no breach in the
friendship of author and publisher, but probably
owing to the "threatened suit in Chancery"
their friendship appears to have terminated. In
1727 Pope vented his indignation without mercy
in "The Dunciad." Lintot and Curll are entered
as rivals in the Race "in honour of the Goddess
of Dulness."

> " But lofty Lintot in the circle rose,
> ' This prize is mine ; who 'tempt it are my foes ;
> With me began this genius and shall end.'
> He spoke, and who with Lintot shall contend ?
> Fear held them mute. Alone, untaught to fear,
> Stood dauntless Curll ; ' Behold that rival here !
> The race by vigour, not by vaunts is won ;
> So take the hindmost Hell,' he said, ' and run.'
> Swift as a Bard the Bailiff leaves behind,
> He left huge Lintot, and outstrip'd the wind.
> As when a dab-chick waddles thro' the copse
> On feet, on wings, and flies, and wades and hops ;
> So lab'ring on, with shoulders, hands, and head,
> Wide as a windmill all his figure spread,
> With arms expanded Bernard rows his state,
> And left-legg'd Jacob[1] seems to emulate."

Nichols says :

" Undoubtedly at this time Pope had con-

---

[1] Jacob Tonson.

ceived a very ill impression of his *quondam* Bookseller. His principal delinquency seems to have been that he was a stout man, clumsily made, not a very considerable scholar, and that he filled his shop with *rubric posts*" ["to which," says D. N. B., "titles of Books in red Letters were affixed."] Dr. Young says that Lintot was a great spluttering fellow liable to fits of rage ("Spence Anecdotes"). "Against his benevolence and general moral character there is not an insinuation."

Soon after this, Bernard relinquished business to his son Henry, and retired to Horsham in Sussex, for which county he was nominated High Sheriff in November, 1735; "an honour which he did not live to enjoy." He died February 3rd, 1735-6, at the age of sixty-one. In the newspapers of the day he was styled "Bernard Lintot, Esq., of the Middle Temple, late an eminent Bookseller in Fleet Street."

Swift said of Bernard Lintot:

> "His character, beyond compare,
> Like his own person large and fair."

HENRY LINTOT,

the only son of Bernard, was born in 1709; he was admitted to the Freedom of the Company of Stationers by patrimony September 1st,

1730. From that time the business was carried
on in the joint names of Bernard and Henry,
but the father passed the principal part of his
time in Sussex. Two days after the death of
Bernard, Henry was appointed High Sheriff for
that county; he resided at South Water, in the
Rape of Bramber, near Horsham. He married
Elizabeth, daughter of Sir John Aubrey, Bart.,
of Llanrtythed, in Glamorganshire, by whom he
had an only daughter and heiress, CATHERINE,
who was married in 1768 (with a fortune of
£45,000) to Captain Henry Fletcher, a Director
of the East India Company. Henry Lintot died
in 1758.

SAMUEL RICHARDSON purchased a moiety of
the Patent of Law Printer in 1760, and carried
on that department of business in partnership
with Miss CATHERINE LINTOT, to whom he left
one of the many memorial rings bequeathed to
his friends. After Richardson's death his widow
and Miss Lintot were for some time joint
patentees.

VI. ROBERT DODSLEY, 1703-1764
JAMES DODSLEY (HIS BROTHER)
1724-1797

OBERT DODSLEY, stocking-
weaver, footman, poet, dramatist,
and publisher, was the son of
Robert Dodsley, who for many
years kept the Free School at Mansfield, Not-
tinghamshire. He was born in the year 1703.
Nichols does not give a biographical account of
him, as he has done of some others of the old
booksellers, but only brief allusions scattered
through the whole series of volumes of his
"Literary Anecdotes." The father of Robert
and James was a man very highly respected in
his neighbourhood, and consequently he had
many pupils from the neighbouring farmers and

ROBERT DODSLEY.

Born in 1703 ; died in 1764.

[To face page 73.

gentlemen. He was a little deformed man; he married a young woman of seventeen when he was seventy-five, and had a child by the union at seventy-eight. Robert was probably the oldest of a large family by a former wife; at all events he was twenty-two years older than his brother Henry.

Not much is known of Dodsley's early days. He is said to have been apprenticed, like William Hutton, to a stocking-weaver, by whom he was so starved and ill-treated that he ran away and entered into the service of Mrs. Lowther: it was in her employment as a footman that he wrote several poems, which were handed about and made much of. He does not appear, in his prosperous days, to have been in the least ashamed of his calling as a footman. When Boswell remarked to Johnson that Dodsley's life should be written, Johnson replied that his brother James (who was then a highly prosperous man) would not thank a man for such a performance; but he added:

"Dodsley himself was not unwilling that his original low condition should be recollected. When Lord Lyttelton's 'Dialogues of the Dead' came out, one of which is between

Apicius, an ancient epicure, and Dartineuf, a modern epicure, Dodsley said to me, 'I knew Dartineuf well, for I was once his footman.'"

Mr. Nichols, in an article on the Rev. Joseph Spence, Prebendary of Durham, and confidential friend of Dodsley, says:

"In a malignant epistle from Curll to Mr. Pope, 1737, Spence is introduced as an early patron of the ingenious Mr. Dodsley:

'Tis kind indeed a *Livery Muse* to aid,
Who scribbles farces to augment his trade;
Where you and Spence and Glover drive the nail,
The Devil's in it, if the plot should fail.' "

These lines refer to a thin octavo volume of poems written by Dodsley which had been published by subscription under the title "The Muse in Livery."

In 1729 he published "Servitude, a Poem": for this work (says the D. N. B.) Defoe is said to have written an introduction in prose. Eighteen months afterwards he brought out a new edition of "Servitude" under the title of "The Footman's Friendly Advice to his Brethren of the Livery, by R. Dodsley, now a Footman." He next composed a dramatic satire, "The Toy Shop," which captivated Defoe, and even Pope received the young footman in a friendly way. The piece was acted at Covent Garden, February 3rd, 1735, with much success.

With the profits derived from the sale of his poems and the result of the performance of his play, he accumulated a small capital, with which, aided by a loan from Pope of £100, Dodsley was enabled to open a bookseller's shop at the sign of "The Tully's Head," Pall Mall, in 1735.

Mr. Austin Dobson, in an interesting article entitled "At Tully's Head," in "Scribner's Magazine" some years ago, says that Mr. Dodsley's shop was on the north side of Pall Mall, next the passage leading into King Street, at present known as Pall Mall Place, or, in other words, about halfway between the Old Smyrna Coffee House of Swift and Prior (the site of Messrs. Harrison's) and the old Star and Garter Tavern.

This was the year in which Jacob Tonson, jun., died, and a few months later died also the famous old Jacob Tonson the elder, whilst early in 1736 Bernard Lintot departed this life. The time of Dodsley's starting in business was therefore very opportune. He had chosen an excellent position, and, as Mr. Dobson says, "he must have opened his campaign as a publisher with considerable vigour."

Pope had evidently great regard for the young publisher, and assisted him not only pecuniarily but by placing several of his works in his hands for publication. In April, 1737, Dodsley published Pope's "First Epistle of the Second Book of Horace Imitated."

The greatest honour conferred on Dodsley, however, and the foundation of his fortune, was the fact that he became the means of introducing the great lexicographer Samuel Johnson to the public as an author.

It was in the year 1737 that Johnson thought of trying his fortune in London, whither, accompanied by his friend and schoolfellow David Garrick, he had journeyed on the plan of "Ride and tie"—one horse between them.[1] He had an introduction to Mr. Cave, publisher of "The Gentleman's Magazine," who found him some literary employment. Johnson told Mr. John Nichols that Mr. Wilcox, the bookseller, on

[1] In my boyhood I have done the same many a time. You ride a mile or so, tie your horse to a gate, and walk on. Your companion following afoot has his turn on horseback, rides a mile beyond you, ties the horse, and so on.

being told by him that he proposed to get his living as an author, eyed his robust frame attentively, and, with a significant look, said, "You had better buy a porter's knot." "He was, however," added Johnson, "one of my best friends."

In April, 1738, Dr. Johnson wrote to Mr. Cave : "I was to-day with Mr. Dodsley, who declares very warmly in favour of the paper you sent him, he desires to have a share in, it being, as he says, 'a creditable thing to be concerned in.'" Boswell said : " It has generally been stated that Johnson offered his ' London' to several book-sellers, none of whom would purchase it." To this circumstance Derrick alludes in the lines of his "Fortune, a Rhapsody" :

> "Will no kind patron Johnson own ?
> Shall Johnson friendless range the town ?
> And every publisher refuse
> The offspring of his happy muse ? "

" But," says Boswell, "the worthy, modest, ingenious Mr. Robert Dodsley had taste enough to perceive its uncommon merit, and thought it creditable to have a share in it. The fact is that at a future conference he bought the whole property, for which he gave Johnson ten guineas."

Johnson's " London " was published anonymously by Dodsley in May, 1738, and astonished the town. " Here is an unknown poet, greater even than Pope," was the first buzz in literary circles.

In 1739 he printed " Manners," a satire by Paul Whitehead, which was voted " scandalous " by the Lords, and author and publisher were ordered into custody, where Dodsley was a week and had to pay £70. Whitehead absconded.

It was in the year 1747 that " Johnson's Dictionary of the English Language " was first announced to the world by the issue of its plan or prospectus. With reference to the origin of this great undertaking, Johnson said that "it was not the effect of particular study, but that it had grown up in his mind insensibly." Mr. Boswell remarks that he had been informed by Mr. James Dodsley that several years before this period, when Johnson was one day sitting in his brother Robert's shop, he heard his brother suggest to him that a dictionary of the English language would be a work that would be well received by the public : that Johnson seemed at first to catch at the proposition, but, after a pause, said, in his abrupt manner, " I believe I shall not undertake it."

Many years afterwards (in 1779) Johnson remarked to Boswell, " Dodsley first mentioned to
me the scheme of an English Dictionary, but I
had long thought of it."—Boswell : "You did not
know what you were undertaking."—Johnson :
" Yes, sir, I knew very well what I was undertaking, and very well how to do it, and have
done it very well."

The production of the great dictionary was
undertaken by Mr. Robert Dodsley, Mr. Charles
Hitch, Mr. Andrew Millar, the two Messrs.
Longman, and the two Messrs. Knapton, and
the price contracted first with Mr. Johnson was
fifteen hundred and seventy-five pounds. (See
" Sketch of Andrew Millar," *ante*, pp. 17, 18.)

In 1748 Mr. Dodsley brought out his " Preceptor " : " One of the most valuable books for
the improvement of young minds," says Boswell,
"that has appeared in any language." To this
meritorious work Johnson furnished " The Preface," containing a general sketch of the book
with a short and perspicuous recommendation
of each article.

In 1751 Dodsley published the first edition
(separately) of Gray's " Elegy."

This year Dodsley brought out Johnson's

"Vanity of Human Wishes," for which Johnson seems to have received fifteen guineas for the right to issue one edition.

In 1749 Dodsley brought out " Irene," for which he paid Dr. Johnson one hundred pounds for the copy, with his usual reservation of the right of one edition. The play ran for nine nights, but mainly, it is said, through Garrick's acting. It is pleasant to learn, however, that Johnson cleared in all nearly three hundred pounds.

Mr. Boswell mentions, with reference to Johnson's celebrated Letter to Lord Chesterfield, that Dodsley, "with the true feelings of trade, said he was very sorry he had written it—for that he had a property in the Dictionary, to which his Lordship's patronage might have been of consequence." He then told Dr. Adams that Lord Chesterfield had shown him the letter. "I should have imagined," replied Dr. Adams, "that Lord Chesterfield would have concealed it." "Poh!" said Dodsley, "Do you think a letter from Johnson could hurt Lord Chesterfield? Not at all, sir. It lay upon his table where anybody might see it. He read it to me; said 'This man has great powers,' pointed out the severest passages, and observed how well they were expressed."

In 1758 Dr. Johnson, in a letter to Bennet Langton, says:

"The two Wartons just looked into the town, and were taken to see Dodsley's 'Cleone,' where David [Garrick] says they were starved for want of company to keep them warm. David and Doddy [Dodsley, author of 'Cleone'] have had a new quarrel, and I think cannot conveniently quarrel any more. 'Cleone' was well acted by all the characters, but Bellamy left nothing to be desired. I went the first night and supported it as well I might: for Doddy you know is my patron, and I would not desert him."

Garrick had rejected it as "cruel, bloody, and unnatural"; Johnson thought there was "more blood than brains in it."

In 1759 Dr. Johnson wrote "Rasselas," and it was published the same year. Mr. Strahan, Mr. Johnston, and Mr. Dodsley purchased it for a hundred pounds; but afterwards paid him twenty-five pounds more, when it reached a second edition.

In 1758 Mr. Spence accompanied his friend Dodsley on a long tour; and on their road paid a visit to the Leasowes, where they were thus noticed by Mr. Shenstone, in a letter to Mr.

Graves : " July 28. Mr. Dodsley and Mr. Spence have been here, and staid a week with me."

His most important achievement was the foundation of " The Annual Register " in 1758, which is still published. Burke was paid a salary of £100 a year for editing it, and was connected with it for thirty years.

Mr. Henry Gray, of East Acton, has been good enough to lend me the original writing of the accompanying receipt for compiling "The Annual Register " for 1768, signed " Thos. English."

Mr. Izaac Reed, in his Preface to Dodsley's " Select Collection of Old Plays," thus speaks of the original editor :

" The first edition of the present volumes was one of the many excellent plans produced by the late Mr. Robert Dodsley, a man to whom literature is under so many obligations, that it would be unpardonable to neglect this oppor- tunity of informing those who may have received any pleasure from the work, that they owe it to a person whose merits and abilities raised him from an obscure situation in life to affluence and in- dependence. Modest, sensible and humane, he retained the virtues which first brought him into notice. . . . He was a generous friend, an en- courager of men of genius ; and acquired the respect and esteem of all who were acquainted with him. . . . After a life spent in the exercise of every social duty, he fell a martyr to the gout, while on a visit to his friend, the Rev. Joseph Spence [author of ' Anecdotes and Characters '], at Durham, in the year 1764, when he had nearly arrived at the age of sixty-one years.

"He was buried in the Abbey Churchyard at Durham, where his tomb is thus inscribed :

" If you have any respect
for uncommon Industry and Merit,
regard this place,
in which are deposited the Remains of
MR. ROBERT DODSLEY,
who as an author raised himself
much above what could have been expected
from one in his rank of life,
and without a learned education ;
and who as a Man was scarce
exceeded by any in Integrity of Heart
and Purity of Manners and Conversation.
He left this Life for a better, September 23, 1764,
In the 61st year of his age."

Amongst the books written by R. Dodsley are the following: "Servitude," published by R. Worrall, 1729; "Footman's Friendly Advice to his Brethren" (this is a new edition of "Servitude "), 1731 ; "A Muse in Livery," 1732 (published by Osborne and Nourse); "The Toy Shop," 1735; "The King and the Miller of Mansfield," 1737 ; "Sir John Cockle at Court," 1738 (sequel to the foregoing); "The Blind

Beggar of Bethnal Green," 1741; "The Public
Register" (Nos. 1 to 24); "Pain and Patience,"
1742; "Colin's Kisses," 1742; "A Select Collection of Old Plays," 12 vols., 12mo, Introduction and notes by Izaac Reed, 1744; "Rex
et Pontifex," 1745; "The Museum," 3 vols.,
1746-7; "The Preceptor," 2 vols., 1748; "A
Collection of Poems by Several Hands," 1748,
3 vols., 12mo; "The Art of Preaching," folio,
n.d.; "Trifles," 1748, with portrait; "The
Triumph of Peace," 4to, 1749; "The World,"
1753-6, 4 vols., folio; "Public Virtue," a
poem, 3 books; "Melpomene, an Ode," 1757,
4to; "Cleone, a Tragedy," 1758; "Select
Fables of Æsop," 1761; "Works of William
Shenstone," 2 vols., 8vo.

Of the foregoing works perhaps the best
known is the "Select Collection of Old Plays,"
12 vols., 1744. In 1758, the year of his retire-
ment from business, he founded "The Annual
Register"—a work which has continued annu-
ally to this day—and the brothers published
Goldsmith's "Polite Learning" the same year.

As regards Johnson's "Rasselas," the D. N. B.
mentions the fact that in "The Grand Magazine
of Magazines" Mr. Kinnersley produced an

abstract of " Rasselas." An injunction was prayed for by the publishers and refused by the Master of the Rolls, on the ground that *an abridgment* is not *piracy.*

JAMES DODSLEY.

(Brother and successor of JAMES DODSLEY.)

JAMES DODSLEY became an active and useful partner to his brother, in connection with whom he published " The Annual Register."

Robert Dodsley quitted business in 1759, but James persevered in acquiring wealth by the most honourable literary connections. In 1788 he was nominated as Sheriff of London and Middlesex, in excuse for which he preferred to pay the customary fees. His property was estimated at about £70,000, which he gave principally to nephews and nieces and their descendants. To some of them £8,000 3 per cents, to others £4,000 or £5,000 in specific sums. His executors were Mr. Thomas Tawney and Mr. John Walter (who had served apprenticeship with his brother Robert); to each of them he left £1,000; to Mr. George Nicoll, £1,000; to Mr. Freeborn, his assistant, £4,000;

to his maid-servant, £500 ; to his coachman, £500, and his carriage and horses.

For many years he kept no public shop, but carried on the business of a wholesale dealer in his own publications only.

Of this stock a large portion was consumed by an accidental fire in a warehouse which was not insured.   He bore the loss without emotion. He kept a carriage many years, but studiously wished that his friends should not know it. Nor did he ever use it east of Temple Bar.

He died February 19th, 1797, aged seventy-four, and was buried in St. James's Church, Westminster.

FROM THE ORIGINAL DOCUMENT NOW IN THE POSSESSION OF MR. HENRY GRAY, EAST ACTON.

[To face page 86.

VII. THE FRIENDS OF LITERA-
TURE

AM indebted to Mr. Robert Bowes of Cambridge for the following interesting account of an old Booksellers' Club. It curiously illustrates the ways and customs of our predecessors of a hundred years ago, and therefore is quite appropriate for insertion in this volume.

At the sale of the Phillipps MSS. I purchased two volumes relating to a society bearing the above name. The first volume is a minute book beginning November 26th, 1805, and ending April 23rd, 1811; the second a collection of letters and receipted accounts. The Friends of Literature were a society of London book-

sellers engaged in the production of trade editions of books; and as these minutes throw
some light on the book trade in the early part
of last century, I have brought together a few
extracts that may interest the booksellers of to-
day.   I give the minutes of the first meeting at
which the Society was formed :

"Queen's Arms Tavern,
"Nov. 26, 1805.
" At a meeting of the following booksellers,
"Mr. John Walker in the Chair,

"Mr. Allen, Mr. John Richardson, Mr. Hood,
Mr. Faulder, jr., Mr. Cuthell, Mr. Ogilvy, jr.,
Mr. Rider, Mr. Harris, Mr. Martin,

" Resolved that we form ourselves into a Society
to be called the ' Friends of Literature.'
" Resolved that every member hereafter request-
ing admittance into this Society, shall be
nominated at one meeting and ballotted for
at the next, two dissentients to exclude.
" Resolved that this Society do meet on the 3rd
Tuesday in every month at 6 o'clock in the
evening; the chair to be taken at 7 o'clock
precisely.
" Resolved that a subscription of one guinea be
paid by each member, at the time of his
admission, into the hands of a Treasurer, to
be hereafter appointed, towards defraying the
expenses of meetings, &c. ; which subscrip-

tion is to be afterwards renewed as often as
necessary.

" Resolved that Mr. Ogilvy, jr., be Treasurer of
this Society.

<table>
<tr><td></td><td>JOHN WALKER.</td></tr>
<tr><td></td><td>ROBIN ALLEN.</td></tr>
<tr><td></td><td>JOSH. FAULDER.</td></tr>
<tr><td></td><td>JAS. RIDER.</td></tr>
<tr><td>Confirmed 21st Jan. 1806.</td><td>JNO. RICHARDSON.</td></tr>
<tr><td>J. WALKER.</td><td>CUTHELL & MARTIN.</td></tr>
<tr><td></td><td>JOHN HARRIS.</td></tr>
<tr><td></td><td>THO. HOOD.</td></tr>
<tr><td></td><td>DAVID OGILVY, JR.</td></tr>
</table>

" Expenses of this meeting, £3 4s. 6d."

And a complete list of the members, with
date of election :

" 1. Mr. John Walker, Nov. 26, 1805 [Paternoster
                                          Row].
2.   Robin Allen   do.   Temple of the
                                          Muses.
3.   John Richardson do.   [Royal
                                          Exchange].
4.   Thomas Hood   do.
5.   Robert Faulder   do.
6.   John Cuthell   do.   Hon. Member
                                   from March, 1808
                                   [Middle Row,
                                          Holborn].
7.   John Harris   do.   St. Paul's
                                          Churchyard.
8.   Peter Martin   do.   retired.

9. Mr. David Ogilvy, jr. do. retired December, 1807.
10.   James Asperne, Jan. 21, 1806 [Cornhill].
11.   James Nunn   do. [Great Queen Street].
12.   Richard Lea   do. [Greek Street, Soho Square].
13.   Edward Jeffery, Feb. 18, 1806 [Pall Mall].
14.   Charles Sharpe, Mar. 18, 1806.
15.   Henry de la hay Symonds, Apr. 15, 1806, retired.
16.   Joseph Faulder, jun., May 20, 1806.
17.   Henry Parry, June 17, 1806 [Leadenhall Street].
18.   Joseph Booker   do. [New Bond Street].
19.   John Murray, April 21, 1807 [Fleet St.]."

The Society was not exclusively a business society, as each meeting was preceded by a dinner. The meetings were usually held, till May, 1808, at the Queen's Arms Tavern; after that date at the New London Tavern, Cheapside. But in the summer the members met at some country inn—the Bull and Bush, North End, Hampstead; the Mermaid, Hackney; and Highbury Barn—and at these meetings there is usually an entry, " No business transacted."

A specimen dinner bill will show the kind of

entertainment : Dinners, £3 18s. ; strong beer,
2s. ; sherry, 12s. ; port, £3 10s. ; dessert, 14s. ;
ingredients, 2s. 6d. ; brandy, 2s. ; tea and coffee,
18s. ; waiters, 5s.—£10 3s. 6d.

The above was probably for thirteen persons,[1]
and as elsewhere the port is put down at 5s.
per bottle, it looks as if each diner consumed a
bottle.   The dinner hour was half-past four or
five, and sometimes a supper followed.

The general constitution of the Society appears from the resolution at the first meeting.
Additional resolutions were passed at later meetings, limiting the total number of members to
a   maximum   of   twenty-five,   and   appointing
certain members to see to the arrangements for
printing, engraving plates, editing, etc.   Mr.
John Walker was elected President, and Mr.
John Harris Vice-President, and no change seems
to have been made during the five and a half
years covered by these minutes.   The number
of members never seems to have reached twenty-
five : two negative votes excluded any new nomi-
nee, and several were proposed but not elected.

[1] Thirteen ! ominous number.   Was there no super-
stition in those days, or did these doughty booksellers
scorn it, like the " Thirteen Club " of to-day ?—E. M.

The works produced by the Society were for the most part entirely divided among the members, but in some cases other booksellers than the members held shares, and in such cases those booksellers were offered an allotment. Of the series known as Walker's Classics, 1,000 copies were withdrawn rateably from the members and divided, 200 to each, to the houses of Johnson, Wilkie and Robinson, Rivingtons, Longman and Co., and Cadell and Davies.

The following are among the works printed by the Society : 4,000 Milton's " Paradise Lost," 4,000 Thomson's " Seasons," by Ellerton and Byworth, in the same manner as the editions sold by Mr. Suttaby, paper to be furnished by Mr. Bonsor at 28s. 6d. per ream, nine months' credit ; 1,000 Bryant's " Mythology," demy (sells 10s. 6d.), by Marchant and Blackader ; 250 ditto, royal (sells 18s.), ditto ; 1,000 West on the Resurrection, with Lyttelton on St. Paul, and Sherlock's " Trial of the Witnesses " ; 5,000 " Robinson Crusoe," demy 24mo, by the Weybridge Press ; 5,000 Young's " Night Thoughts," by the Union Press ; 2,000 Molière, with Bret's Notes ; 1,000 Woodhull's " Euripides," 3 vols., by Blackader ; 50 ditto, large paper,

ditto ; 5,000 " Junius," by W. Wilson ; 5,000
" Telemachus," by Ellerton and Byworth ; 5,000
Chapone and Gregory (?), by W. Wilson ; 5,000
Gay's Fables, by Davidson ; 2,000 Mason on
" Self-knowledge," by Wilson ; Goldsmith's
Essays, Poems, and Plays, Marmontel's Tales,
" Beauties of Sterne."

In the minutes of the meeting of the Society,
October 16th, 1810, the following entry occurs :
" On considering the reduction of the Society,
by the withdrawing of some of the elderly
members, it was agreed to order the dinner in
future for only ten persons."

That points to a decrease in the number of
active members ; and while in the minutes of
the four meetings following the above there was
no resolution to wind up the Society, it is
probable that after April 23rd, 1811, it ceased
to exist.

ROBERT BOWES.

Cambridge, Dec. 5th, 1901.

VIII. BOOKSELLERS' LITERARY CLUB

HE foregoing Club, which Mr. Bowes has almost by accident unearthed, has reminded me of another Literary Club of Booksellers of an earlier date, of which our genial friend John Nichols gave an account, and of which he was himself a happy member.

This pleasant association originated in occasional evening meetings of a few booksellers at the Devil Tavern, Temple Bar. That house having been converted into private dwellings, a regular club was held, once a week, at the Grecian Coffee House.

After a trial of three or four years, the evening club was changed to a monthly dinner at the

"Shakespeare"; and "truly proud," says Nichols, " was honest Campbell, in producing his prime bottles to a Literary Society: whom he justly considered as conferring Celebrity on his house, and to whom he constantly devoted the *Apollo* room." Here it was that Tom Davies first started the idea of writing his " Life of Garrick." At these dinners he frequently produced a small portion of his work, which he would read to them with much complacency.

The actual date of the origin of the Club is not stated by Nichols, but it must have been early in the latter half of the eighteenth century, for the first links of this amiable chain were broken about 1774 by the deaths of Mr. William Davenhill, a young bookseller in Cornhill, of mild and amiable manners, and of Mr. William Davis of Piccadilly," whose learning was profound and his conversation uncommonly brilliant." And among the last survivors was

MR. JAMES ROBSON.

He was born in the year 1733 at Serbergham in Cumberland, where his family had been settled from ancient times in the respectable condition of yeomen. At the age of sixteen he came to London to his relation Mr. Brindley, the eminent bookseller of New Bond Street, to whose business he succeeded in 1759, and as he was a member of the Club for thirty-five years, and was "one of the last survivors," it may be assumed that the Club commenced in the sixties and ended in the nineties of the eighteenth century.

Among other members were Messrs. Alderman Cadell, James Dodsley, Lockyer Davis, Thomas Longman, Peter Elmsley, "honest Tom Payne of the Mewsgate," Thomas Evans, and Thomas Davies. Mr. Robson carried on his business for more than forty years, with integrity, fame, and profit. In 1788, accompanied by his friend Mr. James Edwards, of Pall Mall, he went to Venice on purpose to examine the far-famed Pinelli Library, the catalogue of which made six octavo volumes. This library by a bold and successful speculation he secured. The books were brought to London and sold by auction the following year at the Great Room in Conduit Street.

I have been the more induced to give this brief note of Mr. Robson, because Mr. Nichols tells me that his principal amusement, when relaxing from the tumult of the world, was that which delighted Izaak Walton (and to which I myself am somewhat addicted), and the records of Hampton and Sunbury proclaim his skill and patience as an angler, where, associated with his friend the Rev. Richard Harrison, his medical friend Mr. Woodd, and a few other select companions, he occasionally whiled away the early dawn and evening shade in harmless sport. Though far from being a *bon-vivant* he was a member of the aforementioned club, "a Society," says Mr. Nichols, "which I can scarcely mention without emotion of the tenderest concern, as it brings to mind the many rational hours of recreation it has afforded, when congenial spirits, warmed, not heated with the genial juice of the grape, have unreservedly poured out their whole souls in wit and repartee."

IX. THOMAS EVANS, 1739-1803

R. THOMAS EVANS, whose name is given as a member of the before-named Club, was for some years a considerable bookseller in Paternoster Row, to which situation he advanced himself by industry and perseverance, as he had very little to boast of in point of origin, living when he first came to town with Mr. W. Johnstone, bookseller, of Ludgate Street, in the humble capacity of porter. He afterwards became publisher of "The Morning Chronicle" and "The London Packet," which introduced him to the acquaintance of Dr. Kenrick and several other literary characters, from whose friendship and conversation he obtained much valuable information.

During his publication of the former of these papers a paragraph appeared in it against DR. OLIVER GOLDSMITH, which so highly incensed the Doctor that he was determined to seek revenge ; and no fitter object presenting itself than the publisher, he was resolved all the weight should fall on his back. Accordingly he went to the office, cane in hand, and fell upon him in a most unmerciful manner. This Mr. Evans resented in a true pugilistic style, and in a few moments the author of " The Vicar of Wakefield " was disarmed and extended on the floor, to the no small diversion of the by-standers.

Mr. Evans next succeeded to the business of Messrs. Hawes, Clark and Collins, No. 32, Paternoster Row. By his will, made two years before his death, he bequeathed the bulk of his fortune to MR. CHRISTOPHER BROWN, late assistant to Mr. Longman, and father of Mr. Thomas Brown, for very many years a partner in that house (Nichols's " Lit. Anec.").

The author of " Fifty Years' Recollections of an Old Bookseller " (a work which was published anonymously) was apprenticed to Mr. Evans. His name was Wm. West, as I happen to know

from the fact that in my copy there is appended
an autograph letter addressed to Mr. Collyer,
on presenting him with a copy of his " Recollections." The letter is signed:

"Gratefully and respect^y

" Yrs. WM WEST."

The letter is dated :

" No 1 East Street, West Square Apl 27 '40."

Mr. West gives a long account of Mr. Evans,
with whom he was apprenticed in 1785, or
thereabout, his brother having also been apprenticed to Mr. Evans some years previously.
Evans was a man of very regular habits, strictly
honourable, rigidly punctual in business and of
unceasing industry. If any person in his establishment attempted to cut the string in opening
a parcel, or to use a sheet of new brown paper
in packing one when an old sheet would answer
the purpose, he was severely censured. At the
time when West's brother was apprenticed to
Evans in 1778, his principal assistant was Mr.
John Harris, a gentleman who had been with
him many years ; he possessed very considerable
abilities. After remaining with Mr. Evans for
upwards of fourteen years, he commenced busi-

ness as a bookseller at Bury St. Edmunds ; but
he soon became tired of so dull a life, and returned to his old post for a short time ; but his
disposition and Evans's eccentric habits but ill-
accorded. A separation took place, and for a
short period Harris conducted the business of
the late (that is, the *first*) John Murray—great-
great-grandfather of the present John Murray—
" a gentleman," says West, "of good education
and of considerable tact in that day ; but being
a man of strong passions, as well as of a strong
mind, the irritability of the Scotchman (Murray)
even surpassed that of the Welchman (Evans),
and Mr. Harris gladly made his retreat to a spot
more congenial to his mind, which was the
establishment of the late Mr. Newberry, bookseller, at the west end of St. Paul's Churchyard."
Mr. Harris eventually succeeded to the business,
realized a fortune and retired, leaving the business to his son John Harris. Latterly the business fell into the hands of Grant and Griffiths,
afterwards to Griffiths, Farran and Co.

MR. CHRISTOPHER BROWN,

whose portrait I have pleasure in giving, was a
great and lasting friend of Mr. Evans. Mr.

West says the portrait was from an admirable likeness by John Eckstein, sen.

" Mr. Brown," says " The Old Bookseller," " was of the old school of booksellers, and perhaps there never was an assistant in any establishment that possessed more assiduity and integrity." He seems also to have been, out of business, of a very sociable nature, and it was owing to his cheerfulness, suavity and amiability and considerable humour, that he was chosen a permanent secretary of the society of " Free-and-Easy Counsellors under the Cauliflower," a society which seems to have been conducted with decorum and prudence. It consisted of steady men of business, who " retired from fatigue and enjoyed a glass in moderation, a pipe, and a cheerful song"; and Mr. West well remembered "the vocal powers of Mr. Brown."

" Nursed in the cradle of the wholesale trade, Mr. Brown had been many years an assistant to the late Mr. Thomas Longman of Paternoster Row, until the death of that truly respectable gentleman, by whom he was not forgotten in his last moments for his long and faithful services. He subsequently retired from business at a good old age."

CHRISTOPHER BROWN.

To the Free and Easy Counsellors under the Cauliflower.

From an engraving by J. Eckstein.

[To face page 102.

A few years subsequent to the above period Mr. Evans resigned business in favour of his only son, who was unfortunate, when the whole of the finest and best selected wholesale book connection was handed over to the respectable firm of Messrs. Longmans, Rees and Co.

" Mr. Evans's son, who had married in 1790 a daughter of the second Mr. Archibald Hamilton, had commenced business for himself in his father's lifetime, which he ruined in a few years, deserted his family, and went to America, came back, and died in absolute distress."—NICHOLS's *Lit. Anec.*

X. JOHN NICHOLS, F.S.A., 1744-5-1826

N the compilation of the " Sketches of Booksellers " I have been so much indebted to Mr. Nichols's " Literary Anecdotes of the Eighteenth Century," nine vols., that I am unwilling to quit the subject without devoting space to this most interesting character.

In the sixth volume of his " Literary Anecdotes " he gives a brief and very modest account of his life and work, which occupies about ten pages, and is mainly descriptive of the numerous works written by himself :

" John Nichols, son of Edward and Anne Nichols, was born at Islington, February 2nd,

JOHN NICHOLS, F.S.A.
Born in 1744-5 ; died in 1826.

[To face page 104.

1744-45, and received his education in that village at the academy of Mr. John Shield. In 1757, before he was quite thirteen, he was placed under the care of Mr. Bowyer; who in a short time received him into his confidence, and entrusted to him the management of his printing office.

"In 1766 he became a partner with Mr. Bowyer, who was regarded as the most learned printer of the eighteenth century, with whom in the following year he removed from White Friars into Red Lion Passage, Fleet Street. This union was continued till the death of Mr. Bowyer in 1777.

"In August, 1778, he became associated with Mr. David Kenny in the management of 'The Gentleman's Magazine,' and from that time not a single month elapsed in which he did not contribute several articles to that Miscellany— some with his name or initials, and others anonymously.

"In 1781 he was elected Hon. Member of the Society of Antiquaries at Edinburgh, and in 1785 the same distinction from the Society of Antiquaries of Perth was conferred on him.

"In 1804 he attained what he calls the summit of his ambition, as being elected Master of the Stationers' Company. In 1807 by an accidental fall he fractured one of his thighs; and on February 8th, 1808, his printing office and warehouses, with all their valuable contents, were burnt. Under these accumulated misfortunes, sufficient to have overwhelmed a much stronger mind, he was supported by the con-

solatory balm of friendship and the offer of
unlimited pecuniary assistance, and was enabled
to apply with redoubled diligence to his literary
and typographical labours. In December, 1811,
he withdrew from civic honours, and from a
business in which he had been for fifty-four
years assiduously engaged; and hoping (*Deo
volente*) to pass the evening of his days in the
calm enjoyment of domestic felicity."

He says of himself that he never affected
to posses any superior share of erudition or
to be profoundly versed in the learned languages, content if in plain and intelligible
terms, either in conversation or writing, he
could contribute his quota of information or
entertainment.

Among his numerous literary publications
may be mentioned "Anecdotes, Literary and
Biographical, of William Bowyer," 1778. This
work formed the basis of his "Literary Anecdotes of the Eighteenth Century," 9 vols.,
8vo. In his Advertisement to the ninth and last
volume he says with truth: "It is a mine of
literary materials, whence future biographers and
historians will readily and unsparingly collect
what may suit their several purposes." ("The
History and Antiquities of Leicestershire,"

4 vols., folio.) Mr. Nichols was the author or
editor of sixty-seven separate works.

He died November 26th, 1826. He was well
known to my late partner, Sampson Low.
Among the many friends who contributed to
his "Anecdotes" were Dr. Johnson, Mr.
Steevens, Mr. Cole, Mr. Reed, and his steady
and indefatigable coadjutor, Mr. Gough.

Mr. John Taylor wrote an epitaph on Mr.
Nichols, of which the following is the last
verse :

> "Prompt with good humour all he knew to cheer,
> And wit with him was playful, not severe,
> Such was the sage, whose reliques rest below,
> Beloved by many a friend, without one foe."

Mr. Nichols was not ambitious of exhibiting
fine work as a printer. He left that to Bensley,
Whittingham,[1] and others. Mr. Nichols was
succeeded by his only son, Mr. John Bowyer
Nichols.

The whole set of the nine volumes of the
"Literary Anecdotes" was printed by Nichols,
son and Bentley. I have not discovered when

---

[1] Mr. Whittingham was the founder of the Chiswick
Press, and it is to his successors that I am indebted for
the beautiful typography of this volume.

Mr. Bentley became his partner—at the end of volume six there is an advertisement of works published by Nichols, son and Bentley, of which the following is a brief summary :

I. Critical Conjectures and Observations on the New Testament. By William Bowyer, F.S.A. Fourth edition, one large 4to volume, price £2 7s. 6d., boards.

II. The History and Antiquities of the County of Leicester. Fourth volume. By John Nichols, F.S.A.

III. The Genuine Works of William Hogarth. By John Nichols, F.S.A., and the late George Steevens, Esq., F.R.S. and F.S.A. A new edition in two volumes, demy 4to.   Price £10 10s., boards; or on royal paper, with proof impressions, price £21, boards.

IV. The History of the Worthies of England, endeavoured by Thomas Fuller. First printed in 1662. A new edition, with explanatory notes by John Nichols, F.S.A. 2 vols., quarto, price £5 5s., with a portrait of Fuller.

V. The Works of the Rev. Jonathan Swift,

D.D., arranged by Thomas Sheridan. A new edition corrected and revised by John Nichols, F.S.A., in 19 vols, 8vo, price £9, boards. Also a small edition in 24 vols., royal 18mo, price £4 4s.

VI. Letters on Various Subjects to and from William Nicholson, D.D., with Literary and Historical Anecdotes, by John Nichols, F.S.A. 2 vols., 8vo, price 16s., boards.

VII. The Epistolary Correspondence of Sir Richard Steele. Illustrated with Literary and Historical Anecdotes by John Nichols, F.S.A. 2 vols., 8vo, with a portrait, price 16s., boards.

VIII. Anonymiana, or Ten Centuries of Observations on various authors and subjects. 8vo, price 12s., boards.

IX. The Literary Life and Select Works of Benjamin Stillingfleet, Esq. By the Rev. William Cox, M.A. In 3 vols., price £2 2s. A few copies printed on royal paper, price £3 3s., boards.

X. The Life and Original Correspondence of Sir George Radcliffe, Knt. By Thomas Dunham Whitaker, LL.D.,

F.S.A.   Demy 4to, price £1 1s., or on
royal paper, £1 11s. 6d.

XI. De Motu per Britanniam Civico.   Annis
MDCCXLV et MDCCXLVI.   Liber
unicus. Auctore T. D. Whitaker, LL. D.
12mo, price 6s.

XII. A Trip to Coatham, a watering-place in
the north extremity of Yorkshire.   By
William Hutton, F.A.S.S.   8vo, with a
portrait, map of Cleveland and other
engravings, price 9s.

Mr. Nichols also published many other
works by his old friend William Hutton of
Birmingham, a list of which will be found in
"Sketches of Booksellers of Other Days," page
147.

WILLIAM BOWYER, PRINTER.
Born in 1699 ; died in 1777.

[To face page 111.

XI. WILLIAM BOWYER, 1699-1777

R. WILLIAM BOWYER, Printer,
with whom Mr. John Nichols was
associated from his boyhood, first
as an apprentice and subsequently
as his partner, was the son of William Bowyer,
who was also a printer, and who was born in
1663. He carried on his business at the White
Horse in Little Britain till the year 1699; then
he removed to a house that had formerly been
the George Tavern in Whitefriars. He died in
1737.

In the year 1712-13 the elder Bowyer was in
one fatal night reduced to absolute want by a
calamitous fire. Everyone who knew him was
instant either to relieve or sympathize with him
in his affliction. The younger Bowyer never

forgot this striking testimony of regard for his father.

It was in June, 1722, that William Bowyer the younger entered into the printing business with his father, and so continued till the death of the elder Bowyer in 1737.

I do not propose to give a sketch of the two Bowyers at any length. Mr. Nichols traces the story both of father and son from the birth of the father down to the death of the son ; indeed the story of these two lives forms the basis of his great work, " Literary Anecdotes of the Eighteenth Century," which ultimately extended to nine volumes octavo.

Nichols says of the younger Bowyer that he was confessedly the most learned printer of the eighteenth century. He was born in Dogwell Court, in the extra parochial precinct of White-friars, December 19th, 1699, the year of the great fire which destroyed his father's premises in Little Britain. He may be said to have been initiated from his infancy in the rudiments of the art in which he so eminently excelled. For more than half a century he stood unrivalled as a learned printer, and some of the most masterly productions of this kingdom appeared from his press ; nor was his pen unknown to the world of letters. "The work," says Nichols, "which stamps the highest honour on his name is 'Conjectures on the New Testament,' a book in which the profoundest erudition and the most candid criticism are happily blended."

In 1729 he obtained the office of Printer of the Votes of the House of Commons, which he held for nearly fifty years.

On the death of Samuel Richardson in 1761, he obtained the appointment of Printer to the Royal Society. In 1763 he was nominated Printer of the Journals of the House of Lords and the Rolls of Parliament.

He died in 1777, aged seventy-eight, and was buried in the church of Low Layton in Essex. It was about ten years before his death that John Nichols became his partner.

XII. EDWARD CAVE, Printer
1691-1754

DOCTOR JOHNSON wrote a memoir of Edward Cave for Nichols's "Literary Anecdotes." It occupies the first ten pages of volume v. Cave was not, properly speaking, a bookseller, but as the founder, printer, and publisher of "The Gentleman's Magazine," I have thought it well to include him in these sketches of Johnsonian propagators of literary work.

Dr. Johnson's sketch, so far as it goes, is so admirable, that I must needs avail myself of it largely in what follows.

Edward Cave was born in Newton in Warwickshire, February 29th, 1691. His father

EDWARD CAVE, PRINTER.
Born in 1691 ; died in 1754.

[To face page 115.

was the younger son of Mr. Edward Cave, of
Cave's-in-the-Hole, a lone house, on the street
road in the same county, which took its name
from the occupier; but, having concurred with
his elder brother in cutting off the entail of a
small hereditary estate, by which act it was lost
from the family, he was induced to follow, in
Rugby, the trade of a shoemaker. He lived to
a great age, and was in his latter years supported by his son.

The school of Rugby, in which Edward had,
by the rules of its foundation, a right to be in-
structed, was then in high reputation under the
Rev. M. Holyock, to whose care most of the
neighbouring families — even of the highest
rank—intrusted their sons. He quickly discovered the genius of young Cave, and declared
his resolution to breed him for the university;
but Cave's superiority in literature exalted him
to an invidious familiarity with boys who were
far above him in rank and expectations. When
any mischief was concocted, the fault was sure
to be traced to Cave.

At last his mistress lost a favourite cock.
Cave was with little examination stigmatized as
the thief or murderer; not because he was

apparently more criminal than others, but because he was more easily reached by vindictive Justice.

From that time Mr. Holyock treated him with harshness which the crime in its utmost aggravation could scarcely deserve. Under pretence that Cave obstructed the discipline of the school, by selling clandestine assistance, he was oppressed with unreasonable tasks. Cave bore the persecution for a while, and then left the school and sought other means of gaining a livelihood. He was first placed with a collector of the excise; but the insolence of his mistress disgusted him, and he went to London in quest of more suitable employment, and eventually he was bound apprentice to Mr. Collins, a printer of some reputation, and deputy alderman.

This being a profession suitable to his literary taste, and which furnished employment for his scholastic attainments, he resolved to become a printer, though his master and mistress lived in perpetual discord, and their house was not a particularly comfortable dwelling.

In two years he attained so much skill in his art, and gained so much the confidence of his master, that he was sent without any superintendent to conduct a printing-house at Norwich and publish a weekly paper.

Before the expiration of his apprenticeship his master died, and as he and his mistress could not agree he quitted her house on a stipulated allowance, and married a young woman with whom he lived at Bow. Then he worked as a journeyman with Mr. Barber, a man of some distinction, as a printer for the Tories, and Cave became a writer in "Mist's Journal." He at length obtained an appointment in the Post Office, and was afterwards raised to the position of Clerk of the Franks; his activity in stopping abuses in that department soon made him enemies. He was cited before the House for breach of privilege, and accused of opening letters to detect them, and was, apparently without just cause, ejected from his office.

In course of time he collected a sufficient sum for the purchase of a small printing-office, and began "The Gentleman's Magazine"—a periodical the fame of which is known wherever the English language is spoken. It was to this magazine that he owed the affluence in which he passed the last twenty-four years of his life. It

was a success from the first, and Cave continued
to improve it, till in the year 1751 his wife died
of an asthma.

"He did not seem at first much affected,"
says Mr. Johnson, "yet in a few days he lost
his sleep and his appetite; and lingering two
years, fell by drinking acid liquors, into a
diarrhœa, and afterwards into a kind of lethargic
insensibility, in which one of the last acts of
reason he exerted was fondly to press the hand
that is now writing this little narrative.   He died
Jan. 10, 1754, ætat. 63, having just concluded
the twenty-third annual collection."

He was a man of large stature, tall and bulky,
and of remarkable strength and activity.   He
was generally healthful and capable of much
labour and long application, but in his latter
days he was afflicted with gout, which he endeavoured to cure by abstinence from strong
drinks and animal food.

Dr. Johnson concludes his article with these
words:

"His mental faculties were slow; he saw
little at a time, but that little he saw with great
exactness.   He was long in finding the right,
but seldom failed to find it at last.   His affec-
tions were not easily gained, and his opinion not
quickly discovered: his reserve, as it might hide

his faults, concealed his virtues; but such he was, as they who best knew him have most lamented."

Mr. Nichols "takes the liberty," as he says, "of making some additions to Doctor Johnson's incomparable article."

Mr. Cave had from his earliest printing days conceived the utility of publishing the Parliamentary Debates, but the orders of the House were stringent against the unauthorized publication of these debates. Mr. Cave had somehow contrived to furnish the country printers with certain written minutes of the proceedings in the two Houses of Parliament, which were regularly circulated in the coffee-houses. He was ordered into custody of the Serjeant-at-Arms for supplying his friend Mr. Robert Raikes with the minutes of the House for the use of "The Gloucester Journal." After a confinement of several days, on stating his sorrow for the offence, and pleading that he had a wife and family, who suffered much by his imprisonment, he was discharged with a reprimand on paying the accustomed fees.

In July, 1736, Mr. Cave boldly decided to insert a regular series of Parliamentary debates in

' The Gentleman's Magazine," and his method of proceeding was recorded by Sir John Hawkins :

" Taking with him a friend or two, he found means to procure for them and himself admission into the gallery of the House of Commons, or in some concealed station in the other House : there they privately took down notes of the several speeches, and the general tendency and substance of the arguments. Thus furnished, Cave and his associates would adjourn to a neighbouring tavern, and compare and adjust their notes ; by means whereof and the help of their memories, they became enabled to fix at least the substance of what they had so lately heard and remarked. The reducing this crude matter into form was the work of a future day and of an abler hand : Guthrie the historian, a writer for the Booksellers whom Cave retained for the purpose."

This went on well for two years. Then complaint was made to the House, April 13th, 1738, that the publishers of several news letters, etc., were giving accounts of the proceedings, and it was resolved that it is a breach of the Privilege of this House for any news writer to presume to insert in said letters or papers any account of the Debates, etc., and that the House will proceed with the utmost severity against such offenders.

In February, 1740, Cave committed the care of this part of his monthly publication to Dr. Johnson, who had already given specimens of his ability. In June, 1738, Cave had by way of caution prefaced the Debates by what he called "An Appendix to Captain Lemuel Gulliver's account of the famous Empire of Lilliput," and the Parliamentary Proceedings were given under the title of "Debates in the Senate of Great Lilliput." When Johnson took them in hand the Lilliputian disguise was continued, even beyond the period of Johnson's Debates, which began November 19th, 1740, and ended February 23rd, 1742-3. These Debates were hastily sketched by Johnson when he was not thirty-two years of age, while he was struggling for existence; and yet they had induced learned foreigners to compare British with Roman eloquence.

In 1747 Cave was again ordered into custody of the Black Rod. He begged for pardon and promised not to offend again. Being asked how long he had been a publisher of "The Gentleman's Magazine," he said about sixteen years, since it was first published; that he was concerned in it first with his nephew, and since the death of his nephew he had done it entirely himself.

Being asked how he came to take upon himself to publish "Debates in Parliament," he said he was extremely sorry for it; that it was a very great presumption; that he was led into it by custom and the practice of other people; that there was a monthly book, published before the magazines, called "The Political State," which contained Debates in Parliament; and that he never heard till lately that any persons were punished for printing those books.

Being asked how he came by the speeches which he printed in "The Gentleman's Magazine," he said he got into the House, and heard them, and made use of a black-lead pencil, and only took notes of some remarkable passages, and from memory he put them together himself. Being asked whether he printed no speeches but such as were so put together by himself, from his own notes, he said: "Sometimes he has had speeches sent him by very eminent persons; that he has had speeches sent him by the Members themselves; and has had assistance from some members, who have taken notes of other Members' speeches." Mr. Cave was

discharged with a reprimand on paying his
fees.

On December 7th, 1784, only six days before
Dr. Johnson's death, he sent for John Nichols,
from whom he had borrowed some of the early
volumes of the anecdotes. "Such was the
goodness of Dr. Johnson's heart," says Nichols,
that he solemnly declared "that the only part
of his writings which then gave him any com-
punction was his account of the Debates in
'The Gentleman's Magazine'; but that, at the
time he wrote them, he did not think he was
imposing on the world." The mode, he said,
was to fix upon the speaker's name, then to
make an argument for him; and to conjure up
an answer. He wrote those Debates with more
velocity than any other of his productions.

Mr. Nichols gives many letters from Johnson
to Cave from the earliest date, before his coming
to London, up to the close of Cave's life.

In a footnote to one of these letters, which
by the way are nearly all dateless—with reference
to Johnson's "Life of Savage"—the following
remarks will be found:

"Soon after the publication of this life, which
was anonymous, Mr. Waller Harte, dining with

Mr. Cave at St. John's Gate, took occasion to speak very handsomely of the work. Cave told Harte when they next met, that he had made a man very happy the other day at his house, by the encomiums he bestowed on the author of Savage's Life. 'How could that be?' says Harte; 'none were present but you and I.' Cave replied, 'You might observe I sent a plate of meat behind the screen; there skulked the Biographer, one Johnson, whose dress was so shabby that he durst not make his appearance. He overheard our conversation, and your applauding his performance delighted him exceedingly."

In a conversation with Boswell Dr. Johnson said:

"Cave used to sell 10,000 of 'The Gentleman's Magazine'; yet such was then his minute attention and anxiety that the sale should not suffer the smallest decrease, that he would name a particular person, who he heard had talked of leaving off the magazine, and would say, 'Let us have something good next month!' Mr. Cave's attention to the magazine may indeed truly be termed unremitting; for, as Dr. Johnson once observed to me, 'he scarcely ever looks out of the window, but with a view to its improvement.'"

Here is a specimen of Mr. Cave's poetical abilities, in a billet addressed to a typographical friend:

"Good Master Hughes,
I hope you'll excuse
That a favour to ask I presume ;
What favour is it ?
That me you will visit,
Who cannot stir out of my room.
I hope you are stout
And can trudge about,
And therefore the favour I crave
The sooner the better ;
Thus ends a good letter.
From your humble, *très humble*
E. CAVE."

Mr. Nichols relates the following anecdote of him :

" In the latter part of Mr. Cave's life, having an extensive connection in the line of his business ; at Reading particularly, at Gloucester, and at Northampton, and several relations at Rugby ; he was a frequent traveller ; and time being more an object to him than expence, and the luxury of turnpike roads being then but little known, he generally used four horses. In one of these journeys, calling on an old school acquaintance, a man of great consequence, he directed the servant of the house to inform his master ' that *Ned Cave, the Cobbler,* was come to visit him,' the name by which he was known to his quondam friends at Rugby School, and of which, in his more prosperous days, he was never ashamed."

On Cave's invitation of the Epigrammatists

(to compete for a poetical prize of £50), I find
the following in Nichols's additions to Vol. 5
(vol. viii., p. 511):

> "The Psalmist to a *Cave* for refuge fled,
> And vagrants followed him for want of bread ;
> Ye happy Bards ! would you with plenty dwell,
> Fly to that best of *Caves* in Clerkenwell."

A good portrait of Mr. Cave, by Worlidge,
was inserted in "The Gentleman's Magazine"
for 1754, vol. xxiv., p. 55, and is prefixed to this
"sketch."

There is another portrait of him by Grignion,
with emblemata, devices, and this inscription :

> "EDWARD CAVE, ob. 10 Jan. 1754 ætat 62:
> The first projector of the Monthly Magazines.

> 'Th' invention all admired, and each how he
> To be th' Inventor missed.'"

Mr. Cave was buried in the church of St.
James, Clerkenwell ; but the following inscription to the memory of his father and himself,
which was written by Dr. Hawkesworth, is placed
on a table monument in the north-west churchyard at Rugby :

> "Near this place lies the body of
> JOSEPH CAVE, late of this parish
> Who departed this life Nov. 18. 1747,
> Aged 80 Years

He was placed by Providence in a humble station ;
but
Industry abundantly supplied his wants
and Temperance blessed him with
Content and Health
As he was an affectionate Father
he was made happy in the decline of life
by the deserved eminence of his eldest son
EDWARD CAVE ;
who without interest, fortune, or connections,
by the native force of his own genius,
assisted only by a Classical Education,
which he received in the Grammar School
of this Town,
planned, executed, and established
a literary work called
THE GENTLEMAN'S MAGAZINE ;
whereby he acquired an ample Fortune
the whole of which devolved on his Family
Here also lies the body of Esther his wife,
who died Dec. 30 1734 aged 69 years."